TRUMPOCALYPSE

CONSENT FACTORY ESSAYS
VOL. I (2016-2017)

C. J. HOPKINS

CONSENT FACTORY PUBLISHING

This Consent Factory Publishing trade edition November 2019.

Consent Factory Publishing is a wholly-owned subsidiary of Consent Factory, Inc., a subsidiary of Amalgamated Content, Inc., distributors of quality literary content throughout the developed and developing worlds. For more information about Consent Factory Publishing, visit the Consent Factory's website: consentfactory.org.

Cover design by Anthony Freda.

The essays in this volume were originally published by *CounterPunch* and *Consent Factory*, and republished by *The Unz Review*, *ColdType*, *The Greanville Post*, *OffGuardian*, *ZeroHedge*, *Entelekheia*, *Tlaxcala*, *Oriente Mídia*, *ZNet*, *Burbuja*, *The Fringe News*, *Vocidallestero*, *Public Reading Rooms UK*, *Agora Vox*, *Belligerent Act*, and *Information Clearing House*.

Printed in the United States of America

ISBN 978-3-9821464-0-9 (pb)

"C. J. Hopkins is the rare writer who's so good at identifying uncomfortable truths that he essentially has to be removed from consideration for mass circulation. He's brave, original, enlightening, and hilarious, and his writing has an element of the forbidden that makes it even more fun (you realize later this is also depressing). He's in the tradition of samizdat-type satirists like Voinovich and Mrozek who were early to capture both the horror and absurdity of a collapsing empire."
— Matt Taibbi, Rolling Stone

"History, should there be any, will record 2016 as the year of a stunning triumvirate, the simultaneous eruption of Brexit, Donald Trump, and the Consent Factory. The first two were indications of the deep anguish and anger of common people directed at the neoliberal corporate oligarchy draining the social, economic and political lifeblood from so-called Western democracies. The third was an eruption of brilliant, cutting, incisive satire in the Swiftian tradition, explaining insightfully if painfully what the hell was going on, as the corporate media and its liberal allies desperately counterattacked the populist uprising, a much bigger threat to the oligarchy than the perverted political operatives behind either Trump or Brexit. Here it is to read and remember and to explode the corporate propaganda oozing from the left, right and middle. Trumpocalypse -- you lived it, now understand it."
— John Stauber, author of Toxic Sludge Is Good for You, Weapons of Mass Deception, and other bestsellers

"Is it possible these days to distinguish between political news and satire? Read C. J. Hopkins and see if you can tell the difference. Or rather, enjoy the blend."
— Diana Johnstone, author of Fools' Crusade: Yugoslavia, NATO and Western Delusions, and Circle in the Darkness (Clarity Press, 2019)

ALSO BY C. J. HOPKINS

HORSE COUNTRY

SCREWMACHINE/EYECANDY
(OR HOW I LEARNED TO STOP
WORRYING AND LOVE BIG BOB)

THE EXTREMISTS

ZONE 23

Contents

"In the dark times
Will there also be singing?
Yes, there will also be singing.
About the dark times."
-- Bertolt Brecht

The End of Everything

October 31, 2019

The Trumpocalypse began without warning. No trumpets sounded. There came no Horsemen. No rivers of blood or plagues of locusts. The Lion that is from the tribe of Judah that is also the Lamb with the seven horns and the seven eyes did not appear.

Instead, Donald Trump appeared, in all his aberrant, ignominious glory. He appeared upon a golden escalator, grinning like a used car salesman, jabbering about the death of the American dream, Chevys in China, and "Mexican rapists." Emblazoned on the banner above the stage his minions had installed in the lobby of Trump Tower, and silk-screened onto the T-shirts worn by the "fans" he had paid $50 to be there, lo, the Campaign Slogan of the Beast ...

MAKE AMERICA GREAT AGAIN!

That was June, 2015. The rest, as they say, is history.

Except that history isn't history ... or not what most people think of as history, i.e., a record of things that actually happened, in some sort of factual, verifiable way.

A lot has happened over these last four years ... some of which happened and some of which didn't (depending on your definition of "happened"). Some of what happened actually happened and some of it only officially happened. Some of it probably actually happened, but it didn't officially, and there's no proof that it did, so it might as well have never happened. Some of it definitely actually happened, but it is definitely not what officially happened, so it absolutely never happened, even though we watched it happen. A lot of it was simply made up out of whole cloth, so, obviously, it never actually happened, but it nevertheless officially happened, which caused other things to actually happen (some of which also officially happened), which then caused other things that officially happened (but which obviously never actually happened) to be made up out of whole cloth … and so on.

Four years later, here we are, on the verge of the 2020 elections, and no one knows what the hell is going on. Things are falling apart. The center cannot hold. The blood-dimmed tide is loosed. Et cetera. The Beast is slouching toward Bethlehem. It's pretty much the End of Everything.

How did we ever get to this point?

Well, according to the U.S. Intelligence Community, the political establishment, and the corporate media, shortly after Trump made his announcement, a vast conspiracy of Russians and Nazis suddenly materialized out of the ether and launched an all-out attack on democracy.

Apparently, these Russo-neo-fascists (a/k/a the "Putin-Nazis") had been lying in wait throughout the glorious eight-year Reign of Obama the Beneficent, and now, like a mega-swarm of locusts, they poured up out of their lairs en masse, took to the Internet, and unleashed a veritable blitzkrieg of silly Facebook posts, "discord-sowing" Twitter memes, and other such "divisive" propaganda on the minds of innocent Western consumers.

This Putin-Nazi attack on democracy was discovered by the U.S. Intelligence Community more or less the moment Trump won the nomination,[1] so just as the previous attack on democracy (better known as the Global War on Terror) was winding down after fifteen years.

The Intelligence Community alerted the media, which seamlessly switched from relentlessly flogging the "suddenly self-radicalized terrorist" hysteria that they had been relentlessly flogging for several months to relentlessly flogging Putin-Nazi hysteria.

Which is more or less where I came in.

*

1 *Actually, it began even earlier than that, with the Brexit referendum in Great Britain, which the corporate media later discovered had been orchestrated by the Putin-Nazis, who had brainwashed millions of British subjects into voting to leave the European Union, but that wouldn't be "discovered" until later.*

Back in the summer of 2016, like most other halfway rational people, I regarded the candidacy of Donald Trump as some sadistic cosmic joke the gods were playing on anyone foolish enough to believe in American electoral politics. This was, after all, Donald Trump, the B-List celebrity billionaire buffoon who went around plastering his name on everything in big, gold, shiny, ostentatious letters ... hotels, casinos, country clubs, you name it. He put his name on steaks for Christ's sake. The man even had a fake university. His "candidacy" was clearly a promotional prank. He was probably preparing to launch a line of Trump-branded condoms on QVC, or a New York Times bestseller, or something.

Also, everyone understood that Hillary Clinton had been appointed to carry on the works of Obama the Beneficent, who had saved democracy from the 2007-2008 financial crisis caused by irresponsible borrowers and greedy low-level service employees, and who had single-handedly eradicated racism, and had established everlasting peace on Earth by mercilessly bombing the Middle East, assassinating various "terrorists" and their families, and just generally being a living, breathing avatar of hope and change. The election was a mere formality.

Given the horrors of these last four years -- the Russian occupation, the concentration camps, the annexations of Canada and Mexico, and all the other Trumpocalyptic horrors -- it's hard to remember back to those heady days when Americans were happy and free. OK, sure, many of them had lost their houses when they couldn't keep up with the vig on the extortionate loans that they had taken out to desperately try to make ends meet when they couldn't keep up with the vig on their credit cards, which they had maxed out trying to make ends meet after paying the vig on their student loans, and their kids' student loans, and doctor bills, and so on, after their jobs got offshored to Mexico and China ... but at least they could still curl up at night in their parents' basements secure in the knowledge that the president was an African American, and the next one was going to be a woman.

That was the important thing, after all. That, and ... well, the S&P Index. And the continuing health of Goldman Sachs, Citigroup,

Credit Suisse, JPMorgan Chase, BofA Securities, Morgan Stanley, Deutsche Bank, and other important financial institutions. That, and the projected earnings of Pfizer, Johnson & Johnson, Raytheon, Boeing, Amazon, Google, and ExxonMobil.

As long as the global economy was thriving, and investors were happy, Americans were happy. So what if they had to work twice as long for half the pay at demeaning McJobs to enrich a supranational cartel of corporations, politicians, emirs, oligarchs, bankers, celebrities, and their coteries of ruthless personal assistants? As long as global capitalism was spreading democracy throughout the world, and keeping those terrifying terrorists at bay, and Obama, or Clinton, or some other smirking icon of wokeness was in the White House, what was there to complain about?

Well ... quite a lot, apparently. Or at least that's what the godless Rooskies brainwashed millions of ignorant hillbillies and African Americans into believing with their insidious, mind-controlling Facebook ads.[2] You wouldn't have known it from reading the papers or watching CNN or MSNBC, but beneath the veneer of smiley, happy, hopey-changey Obamamerica, a maelstrom of discontent was brewing.

Back then, in the spring of 2016, I was trying to finish a dystopian novel I had been trying to finish for several years. I had mostly been ignoring electoral politics, and I had planned to continue doing just that. I'm not allowed to vote here in Germany, and I've never found the ins and outs of deciding exactly which corporate puppets get elected back home to be all that fascinating.

What caught my attention was Bernie Sanders, or, rather, the corporate media's efforts to delgitimize him and destroy his candidacy. I pulled up the *New York Times* one day, and there was Paul Krugman performing feats of sophistical magic to turn Sanders into a racist.[3] I pulled up *The Guardian*, and, lo and behold, a bright, young journalist named Lauren Gambino (who would go on to cover the Clinton campaign as if Hillary was personally paying her salary) was lexically bombing the bejesus out of Bernie and his "rabble rousing"

---

2 "Russian trolls chief target was 'black U.S. voters' in 2016," BBC News, October 9, 2019

3 Krugman, Paul, "The Pastrami Principle," The New York Times, April 15, 2016

so-called "Bernie Bros."[4] I skimmed the corporate press a bit further. Yes, it appeared the punditocracy was out to get him, in a systematic fashion.

Not that Bernie was a real threat to anything (as he would later demonstrate by campaigning for Clinton, rather than running as an independent, after she and her cronies crushed his "revolution"), but he was riding a rising wave of populist anger at the American neoliberal establishment and the venal political class that serves them. Americans, it seemed, had finally had enough of the Democratic Party's fake-left con, and they were looking for some actual hope and change ... or at least some semblance of social democracy, like publicly subsidized universal healthcare and affordable university education, which every other Western country has provided to its citizens for years.

Anyway, I did a bit more looking around, and it turned out this wave of populist anger was not exclusively an American phenomenon. While I'd been lost in my little fictional world, out in the real world, something was shifting. In the U.K., the flagship of European austerity, a date for the E.U. Referendum had been set. Corbyn was leading the Labour Party, much to the displeasure of the neoliberal Blairites. In France, support for Hollande was plummeting; support for Le Pen and Mélenchon was rising. Here in Germany, the AfD, Pegida,[5] and other neo-nationalist right-wing populist movements were growing. In Italy, Spain, Hungary, Austria, Greece, anywhere you looked in Europe, left- and right-wing populism was taking on the neoliberal establishment.[6]

---

4 Gambino, Lauren, "Bernie Sanders rally in New York strikes at heart of establishment," The Guardian, April 14, 2016

5 An abbreviation of "Patriotische Europäer gegen die Islamisierung des Abendlandes" (i.e., "Patriotic Europeans Against the Islamisation of the Occident"), as "Gestapo" was an abbreviation of "Geheimstaatspolizei." Seriously, this is the actual name these geniuses chose for their Muslim-hating group. I guess "Citizens for a Racially Pure Germany" was taken.

6 The fact that the vast majority of this challenge was initiated by the neo-nationalist Right does not prove that the people whose anger these right-wing forces are exploiting are a bunch of fascists. It proves that the Left (with several notable exceptions) have, since at least the 1960s, wedged themselves so far up the asses of the global capitalist ruling classes, and ignored the actual working classes (or worse, demonized them as racists when they failed to embrace identity politics), that they had forfeited the ability to represent them. Some elements on the Left are addressing this, finally, but at this point the damage is so extensive that it's going to take years to rebuild trust ... that is, if the Left is even capable of abandoning identity politics and the destructive atomization of the working classes.

This populist backlash against the juggernaut of global capitalism and its ideology was inevitable, but I hadn't expected it so soon. Honestly, I didn't think I'd live to see it happen. I'd figured it was decades off in the future, which it may still be, depending on what happens during the next few years. It all comes down to how successfully the global capitalist empire and its goons can put down the current populist insurgency. A little history is probably in order here, to put that in context. I'll try to do it quickly.

Ready? OK, here we go ...

*

Back in the early 1990s, the Soviet Union finally fell apart, and the last ideological adversary to global capitalism disappeared. We haven't been able to adequately get our minds around the significance of that yet, but, basically, what happened was, supranational capitalism (not the United States of America) became the first globally hegemonic empire in the history of aspiring hegemonic empires. Neither the Babylonians, nor the neo-Babylonians, nor the Persians, the Romans, the Holy Romans, the Macedonians, the Austro-Hungarians, the Rashidun Caliphate, the Yuan Dynasty, not even the Mongols or the British Empire, nor any empire in the history of ... well, history, has dominated the entire planet, until now.

Being supranational in nature, it is an empire unlike any other empire. It is an empire, not only without an emperor, but without any borders, or territories (or, rather, being globally hegemonic, it contains all territories within itself, and thus renders the concept of "territory" meaningless). It is an empire without external adversaries, because there is no external territory from which an adversary can launch an attack, either a physical or an ideological attack. Its ideology is the only ideology. Thus, it is no longer ideology.[7] It has transcended ideology and become "normality," or, in other words, simply "the way it is."

---

7 There is no longer a competing ideology with the power to call it "ideology." Ideology is not just a bunch of beliefs. Ideology needs a functioning material power structure to legitimize it, to render it "normative" throughout a society. Cults, for example, don't have ideologies. Their belief systems are deviations from ideology, i.e., the normative belief system they exist within.

To understand this, one has to let go of seeing things in terms of nations competing (or warring) against other nations to defend or increase their power as nations. Capitalism couldn't care less about nations. Neither do the capitalist ruling classes, except for the value they have as assets (i.e., the U.S. military) or as liabilities (i.e., Iraq, Libya, Syria, et cetera). Do you seriously believe that bailing out the Wall Street banks back in 2008 had anything to do with helping Americans, or that the restructuring of the Greater Middle East (and, of course, the former Soviet Bloc) is being carried out to benefit Americans, or the citizens of any other nation?

I guarantee you, it is not.

Not that nations don't still exist. Of course they do. And, naturally, they compete with each other for various advantages ... just as corporations do. But what they do not do (what they no longer do) is attack or challenge global capitalism, or its fundamental ideology.

They do not do this (i.e., challenge global capitalism or its omnipresent ideology) because the economies of every developed nation on Earth are totally interdependent (or they are dependent on ones that are interdependent). The People's Republic of China owns over $1.3 trillion of U.S. debt, so that its currency, the yuan, stays pegged to the dollar, so that the U.S. stays its largest export market. Russia relies on German imports. Germany relies on Russian oil and gas. The British economy relies on everyone. And everyone relies on the Saudis.

This is why, despite all the "Russia" hysteria we've been subjected to over the last three years, the U.S. is not going to war with Russia. The U.S. does not want to conquer Russia. *Global capitalism wants to re-globalize Russia.* It wants to open Russia back up (like it was doing during the 1990s, when Russia's leader was a drunken Western puppet). It wants to privatize and restructure Russia, and China, and the Greater Middle East, and every other country and territory that it hasn't already restructured and privatized, stripped of its non-capitalist cultural values, and absorbed into the global market.

This is all capitalism knows how to do. This is what it exists to do. It is, in essence, ideologically speaking, a values decoding/recoding machine, one that strips societies of their non-capitalist values (i.e., religious, traditional, sociocultural, and other such despotic values) and replaces them with a single value ... exchange value, thus rendering everything and everyone an interchangeable commodity.[8]

Once it has achieved this mission (i.e, rendering everything essentially valueless, interchangeable, and utterly meaningless), capitalism is more than happy to sell the empty husks of people's sociocultural values back to them in the form of "identities" and "lifestyle choices," which pose no threat whatsoever to capitalism. On the contrary, as far as capitalism is concerned, the more identities and sub-identities the better. The more thoroughly a society can be atomized into market demographic niches, the more manageable and exploitable it becomes. As long as everyone conforms their actual behavior to capitalist ideology (i.e., works a job, pays their debts, believes in private property, and so on), they can "be" whatever they want to "be." Christians, Muslims, socialists, anarchists, gay, cisgender, trans, nonbinary, ecofeminist paleoconservative vegans living off the grid, Satan-worshipping Trotskyite furries ... capitalism couldn't care less.

What does pose a threat to global capitalism, and what is posing a threat to global capitalism currently, is people attempting to defend, preserve, or reassert their non-capitalist values and subjugate global capitalism to them. It does not matter one iota whether these values are progressive or conservative. If they threaten to restrict the power of global capitalism to render everything a commodity, they must be delegitimized, and dealt with harshly.

The socialist who wants to abolish private property (or even the social democrat who wants to reregulate the Wall Street banks, nationalize the healthcare system, subsidize university education, and provide a basic "safety net" for each and every member of society) is elevating societal welfare above the welfare of the capitalist market. The fundamentalist Christian who wants to ban abortion, or have the choice not to bake gay wedding cakes, is elevating Christian morality above the amorality of the capitalist market. Both the socialist and the fundamentalist Christian are free to hold their respective values, but they are not free to attempt to actually live their lives

8 "Despotic" meaning "arbitrary" (rather than "tyrannical" or "autocratic"), i.e., determined and enforced by an act of will, whether the will of a leader or social group, as opposed to being legitimized by "science," "natural law," or some other type of unchallengeable "a priori truth." I go into all this at greater length in Tomorrow Belongs to the Corporatocracy, one of the essays in this collection, which many of my readers found quite depressing.

according to these values. If they try, they will be dealt with harshly.

Or take, for example, two Islamic theocracies ... the Kingdom of Saudi Arabia and the Islamic Republic of Iran. One is playing ball with global capitalism; the other, for the most part, is not. Global capitalism couldn't care less how the Saudi royals oppress their subjects, or if they finance a little terrorism now and then, as long as they're playing their part in the empire. Iran, on the other hand, is a major problem, and is a member of the "Axis of Evil," not because it is any more theocratic or oppressive than the Kingdom of Saudi Arabia, but because it will not acknowledge and surrender to the empire. The Iranians (like those godless Rooskies, and Venezuela, Syria, and other problematic countries) are behaving as if there were no empire, as if the world was still comprised of sovereign nations that could do whatever they wanted.

*

Which brings us back to that populist backlash against global capitalism and its ideology. See, regardless of whether working people think about all this stuff consciously or not, they feel the global capitalist empire. They feel its presence ... its omnipresence. They feel its emptiness. They feel its pointlessness. They feel it at the mall, alone in their cars, staring into the screens of their smartphones as they stagger down the street like zombies. They feel it thumbing through online ads for anti-depressants and potential sex partners. They feel it in their corporate cubicles and in the chill-out areas of their corporate campuses and in the aisles of their corporate supermarkets stocked with seventy brands of toothpaste and taste-free, genetically-modified produce individually wrapped in plastic. They feel it in the thoughts they cannot think and in the dreams they can no longer remember. They feel it everywhere, because it is everywhere, stripping away the last shreds of their values, restructuring, privatizing, commodifying everything. They may or may not be able to name it, or explain it, but they feel the empire. You feel it, don't you? I certainly do.

Anyway, by the summer of 2016, a lot of people were tired of feeling it. The British people were so tired of feeling it that they voted to leave the European Union. Americans had gotten so tired of feeling it that they elected Donald Trump president that November. I know it's hard, but try to remember back to what a joke this was, to how ridiculous and totally inconceivable this was ... that Donald Trump could be elected president.

Americans did this. They did this knowingly. They elected a completely politically unqualified, clinically narcissistic, borderline moronic, word-salad-babbling ex-game show host who boasted of "grabbing women by the pussy" and was promising to build "a big beautiful wall" to keep out the imaginary hordes of Mexican rapists that were storming the border. Americans knowingly walked into their polling stations and elected this ass clown, not because they had been brainwashed by the Russians, not because they had suddenly morphed into a bunch of Hitler-loving white supremacists, but because they were utterly exasperated with the empire and its soulless ideology, and its simulation of democracy, and above all its political stooges, and they saw a chance to toss a massive stink bomb into establishment headquarters ... a stink bomb by the name of Trump.

In case it wasn't clear by now, I'm not a fan of Donald Trump, nor am I a fan of the Democrats. I'm not a cheerleader for either party. I started writing and publishing the essays in this series in reaction to the global capitalist ruling classes' reaction to this populist backlash that I sensed fairly early might be going on.[9] My focus is on the empire itself, and its propaganda ministry, the corporate media, and the ideological counter-insurgency they have been waging for the last three years.

Sitting here, in October of 2019, reflecting back on everything that has happened (or hasn't happened, officially or otherwise), recalling all the incremental, seemingly laughable, insidiously effective, choreographed steps that have led us to this point, it appears that counter-insurgency is working.

9 All of the essays in this first volume originally appeared in CounterPunch, and on the Consent Factory blog, which I launched that spring. Later, they were also republished by The Greanville Post, The Unz Review, ColdType, OffGuardian, ZeroHedge, and many other alternative outlets on both sides of the political spectrum, or maybe both extremes of the political spectrum. I'm publishing the best of them in this series: (a) because I'm old, so I don't trust the Internet; and (b) to add to the historical record of just how batshit crazy things got.

We are drowning in a sea of manufactured mass hysteria, official propaganda, fabricated news, and just bull goose loony conspiracy theories. Celebrity former Intelligence officials posing as political analysts bark out at us from our televisions nightly, assuring us that "America is under attack!" Generals write op-eds in *The New York Times* more or less calling for a military coup. The Department of Homeland Security monitors social media for "divisive content." Neo-McCarthyite mania reigns. Anyone deviating in any way from the empire's new official narrative is either a "fascist" or a "Russian asset." Gradually, methodically, over the course of three years, the ruling classes have whipped the Western masses up into a mindless frenzy of full-blown Putin-Nazi paranoia ... and now, somewhere in the bowels of the Capitol, a secret impeachment is underway.

The way I see it, one way or another, the global capitalist ruling classes are going to do away with Donald Trump (and Brexit, which will either never happen or will happen in some purely nominal way). They will do this during 2020, either by forcing him out of office like Nixon, or by jacking up the mass hysteria and Putin-Nazi paranoia to the point where Americans will vote him out of office simply to make the madness stop. That, or maybe they'll have to kill him.[10]

Or, maybe I'm wrong, and it isn't working ... the global capitalist ruling classes' counter-insurgency, their War on Populism. Maybe we really are on the brink of a second civil war, as so many believe. Maybe this is really the End of Everything, the Trumpocalypse, and Trump will get reelected, or he won't, so he'll burn down the Capitol Building (and blame it on "the Mexican Communists," of course), declare martial law, appoint himself Führer, and unleash his legions of Russia-loving, American flag-waving white supremacists (with tactical support from the "New Red Army") on whatever remains of the neoliberal "Resistance." Or something more or less along those lines, or possibly even more Trumpocalyptic. No one knows how this is all going to end.

In any event, here's how it started ...

---

10 Or, rather, discover him in the Lincoln Bedroom, having violently strangled himself to death, and then hung himself from the bedposts with a sheet, like Mark Epstein. Stranger things have happened.

America Saves the World Again!

June 3, 2016

So, Donald Trump, the billionaire buffoon, and latest official Hitler-alike, wants to "Make America Great Again," and neoliberal elites throughout the world are noisily soiling themselves en masse in the mainstream press on a daily basis.

According to respected, prize-winning papers like *The New York Times*, *The Washington Post*, *The Guardian*, and some other less prize-winning sources, we're looking at pretty much the end of the world here … which only Hillary Clinton can save us from.

Seriously, Nobel Prize-winning economists like *The Times'* Paul Krugman are down in the trenches taking shots at Clinton's opponents like a bunch of common PR hacks. *The Washington Post* is on the verge of setting some kind of Guinness world record for hit-pieces on both Trump and Sanders, although Sanders has been their primary target. *The Guardian,* in addition to belittling Sanders at every opportunity throughout the primaries, and flogging the coming global Trumpocalypse, has been churning out Clinton testimonials and Obama hagiographies at a blinding pace. Their latest was a heart-warming photo exposé of Obama playing basketball, fist-bumping a janitor, and letting some little kid touch his head. *The Telegraph* has broken out the Riefenstahl references. *The Times* brought in an authentic German to make the Weimar Republic analogy. And the primaries aren't even over yet.

These are just a few of many examples from what we're supposed to think of as "respectable" broadsheets. The tabloids, television, online magazines, leading politicians, global business leaders, beneficent oligarchs and other "opinion makers," and the rest of the neoliberal establishment, are freaking out about how their quadrennial simulation of democracy is unfolding. It seems the center cannot hold, or some rough beast is slouching toward ... something.

Which means it's time for another episode of America Saves the World Again! (The working title of this popular series was Capitalism Saves the World Again!, but that didn't fly with the test-screening audiences.) If you don't immediately recognize this show, here's a quick recap to jog your memory.

This show has been running for about seventy years. It's an action-based show, so the premise is simple. The way it works is, in the opening episode of whatever season we're currently watching, the protagonist, America, is called upon to save the "free world," and democracy, and so on, from some megalomaniacal fascist antagonist. The name and face of the antagonist changes (depending on who we need to demonize), but he's always megalomaniacal and fascist, and oddly reminiscent of Hitler.

In the early seasons, the theme was always America versus the Communist Menace, so there was kind of a dual-antagonist thing going. The main antagonists were the Soviets, of course, Stalin, at first, then all his successors. Guest antagonists included Kim Il-sung, Fidel Castro, Ho Chí Minh, Rafael Ureña, Daniel Ortega, Manuel Noriega, and some lesser lights, each of whom was just like Hitler, or kind of like Hitler, or ... well, close enough. They milked this angle for forty-four years, right up until the end of the Cold War.

Sometime circa 1989, after America had saved the world from the Evil Empire of Communism, the show-runners started to change things up. Still, the antagonist is always Hitler, or someone very much like Hitler, only now without the Communism angle (Genocide and Terrorism have been the standard themes).

The post-Cold War line-up of "baddies" has featured Saddam Hussein, Slobodan Milošević, Osama bin Laden, Mohammed Omar, Saddam Hussein again, Muammar Gaddafi, and an assortment of terrorists whose names I forget. The Iranians don't appear to be Hitler, currently. The Russians, however, are making a comeback.

I'm pretty sure you recognize this show by now.

So what's the deal, you're probably asking, with this endless series of Hitler-alikes that America is always saving the world from? The answer has to do with mythology, mostly.

See, every empire has a founding myth, and saving the world from Hitler is ours. By "ours," I don't mean just Americans. I mean every citizen of the American Empire, which came into being in 1945. I mean everyone living under global capitalism, beginning from the end of the Second World War.

Now we need to back up a bit to understand this, because World War II was not just any large-scale war for territory and resources, control of markets and trade routes, et cetera. It *was* that, of course, but we can also understand it as the last attempt of despotism to turn back the tide of transnational capitalism, which, prior to the outbreak of war, was in a particularly laissez-faire phase ... a phase sort of like the one we're in now.

By the early years of the 20th Century, industrialization, globalization, free trade, liberalism, democracy, and so on, had radically shifted the balance of power from the titled (i.e., despotic) nobility to the merchant (i.e., capitalist) classes. I'm over-simplifying for the sake of brevity, but basically what was going on (i.e., with World War I, the "Roaring Twenties," the Great Depression, the hyperinflation in Germany, and the rest of the chaos the world was experiencing) was the death throes of the old imperial world order, and the birth of the global capitalist world order ... which was going to need to be managed by someone.

As it turned out, the U.S.A. was that someone.

By 1945, so the end of World War II, the last of the great European empires that had pretty much run things since the 15th Century had either been crushed (i.e., Austria-Hungary, Germany a/k/a the Holy Roman Empire, the Ottoman Empire, Russia, et al.) or reduced to husks of their former selves (i.e., the British Empire, France, Spain). Nazi Germany and the Empire of Japan were desperate attempts to resurrect the nationalist or race-based type of imperium that modern capitalism had already dismantled.

This was the end of despotism as a viable imperial power structure. It would take another forty-four years for fake communism in the U.S.S.R. to run its course, but it was doomed from the start, or from the moment it abandoned its global aspirations.

In any event, a new empire was born ... an entirely different type of empire. An empire with an American face, and whose enforcement arm was the U.S. military, but whose nature was always essentially transnational.

In other words, borrowing from Paddy Chayefsky, and Mr. Jensen's speech near the end of *Network*, "There is no America. There is no democracy. There is only IBM, and ITT, and AT&T, and DuPont, and Dow … those are the nations of the world today."

One quick example to make my point, then I'll get right back to the mythology thing. Look at what "America" has been doing since the end of the Cold War and ask yourself: whose interests does all this serve, exactly?

According to a lot of mainstream pundits, the invasions of Iraq, the bombing of Libya, and our destabilization of other countries, have all been disastrous failures for "America," as is much of our current foreign policy. Which is true, if one defines "America" as a sovereign nation comprised of citizens, whose government exists to serve their interests. If that's the way you define America, then most of U.S. foreign policy makes absolutely zero sense.

On the other hand, if you understand "America" as the symbolic face of transnational capitalism, then suddenly everything *does* make sense. The chaos the U.S.A. has been sowing throughout the Middle East, on Russia's borders, and in other quarters throughout the world, is all part and parcel of capitalism's ongoing mission to expand and exploit new markets, and to do away with the final remnants of any despotic structures and values that stand in the way of its dominance of … well, everything.

Looking at things this way, it is also clear that actual Americans (i.e., American citizens) mean nothing more to global capitalism than actual Iraqis, Yemenis, Mexicans, or the citizens of any other nation-states … which possibly sheds a little light on recent trends in the U.S.A., like the mysteriously disappearing middle-class, or why a nation would allow its banks to debt-enslave its university students, and anyone else they can get their hooks into, in order to enrich a transnational elite of investors who have no loyalty to anything.

Which brings us back to our founding myth, and America Saves the World Again! See, the picture I just painted above is terribly depressing, and unromantic, and makes it hard for global Capitalism to sell itself as "freedom," "democracy," "progress," and all that other stuff. It also makes it extremely difficult to keep people thinking in terms of nations, and "our national interests," and "threats to the nation." People, once they start to see things clearly and realize that their "national leaders" couldn't give two shits about them, get really angry, which is inconvenient. So capitalism needs to distract them somehow, and redirect their anger somewhere, and give them something to believe in again.

Fortunately, for global capitalism, what usually works is a reenactment of its founding myth (i.e., saving the world from the original Hitler, nevermind that it was actually the Russians who did the heavy lifting on the Eastern Front.) These reenactments are almost always effective, as they tend to get folks all riled up, and ready to believe almost any kind of ridiculous nonsense the neoliberals are peddling … like the Iraqi Weapons of Mass Destruction hoax, or the one about the Kuwaiti babies being yanked out of their incubators.

Or the story being peddled to us now ... the one where Donald Trump plays Hitler, and is threatening the very fabric of democracy, and possibly the existence of all life on the planet, and only Hillary Clinton and her friends at Goldman Sachs can save us.

That is, of course, unless Clinton blows it, which isn't completely out of the question. In which case the boys at Goldman Sachs, the WEF, the Council on Foreign Relations, and the other folks who are actually running things — the Mr. Jensens of the world — will need to have one of those "talks" with Trump, like the one they had to have with Reagan back when he was a populist demagogue.

Whatever happens, we can all look forward to another exciting Summer Season of America Saves the World Again! Personally, I'm looking forward to the episode wherein Bernie Sanders leads his Sandernistas into the hills to prepare for revolution, or breaks their hearts by supporting Clinton, despite everything he's been saying about her, which he'll explain he has no choice but to do, and will encourage them to do, because … you know, Hitler!

I don't want to spoil the suspense or anything, but I think you know how that one turns out.

The Blood-Dimmed Tide of Neo-Nationalism and Other Scary Simulacra

June 12, 2016

Well, it's shaping up to be a long, hot Summer, or year, or possibly decade or two, what with all the global political chaos, racial tensions, social unrest, and the blood-dimmed tide of neo-nationalism rising inexorably out of Spiritus Mundi like the contents of a backed-up toilet. Whatever is actually going on — which is probably not as apocalyptic, but more insidious and dystopian than it seems — the worst are certainly full of passionate intensity. Based on the miasma of mindless hysteria being pumped out by the corporate media, and then endlessly echoed on Facebook and Twitter, you would think the end of days was nigh. Or at least the end of Western civilization, or democracy, or America, or capitalism … or something.

Nothing could be further from the truth.

The fact is, for the global capitalist ruling classes, the transnational corporate and deep-state elites — the folks who are actually running the show, to the extent that anyone is actually running it — things couldn't be going much better at the moment. Sure, for the vast majority of us, the future is looking increasingly miserable, but try to see things from their perspective. Here we are, barely twenty-five years since the dissolution of the last real impediment to their domination of … well, pretty much everything, and just look at all they've managed to accomplish.

The Greater Middle East has been successfully destabilized. Iraq, Afghanistan, Syria, Libya, any country not playing ball with transnational capitalism has been brought to its knees by a series of invasions, bombings, sanctions, support for insurgencies, corruption, et cetera. Iran is currently negotiating in the hope of avoiding a similar fate. Russia, following its transformation into an autocratic capitalist free-for-all for ex-KGB men and their oligarch cronies — a transformation designed by folks like Jeffrey Sachs, Lawrence Summers, the Harvard Institute for International Development, the IMF, and other shock therapists — has been more or less surrounded by the EU and NATO, and is being pressured to get with the program. China, in spite of its playing grab-ass with the U.S. Navy in the South China Sea, is deep into the global capitalism thing. Vietnam and Laos have joined the club. Cuba is even opening for business again. South America is a work-in-progress, as ever, what with the recent neoliberal "soft" coup in Brazil, the re-neoliberalization of Argentina, the destabilization of Venezuela, and so on.

This is just a quick summary of the highlights. The point is, apart from some isolated pockets of resistance, which the corporatists will get to eventually, and the various nightmarish terrorist theme parks operating out in the imperial hinterlands, it's one big global capitalist world, one Market under Mammon, indivisible, with privatization and austerity for most, and distractionary paranoia for all.

The Simulation of National Sovereignty

One of the most effective ways the global capitalist ruling classes distract us from the fact that they are transforming the entire planet into a combination shopping mall/labor camp is the simulation of national sovereignty. Most of us, since the late-18th Century, have been conditioned to perceive the world as a competition between sovereign nations, each pursuing its own national interests. Which, of course, it is to some extent. However, as we have all been experiencing, sovereignty isn't what it used to be. JPMorgan Chase, ICBC, HSBC, Berkshire Hathaway, Royal Dutch Shell, AXA Group, Toyota, Exxon, Pfizer, Novartis … does anyone believe these transnational banks and corporations have any real allegiance to the "sovereign nations" they nominally reside in, or to the citizens of those "sovereign" nations? No, and yet we go on perceiving and discussing things as if they did.

We talk about the foreign and domestic policies of the government of the United States as if they had been intended to somehow benefit the "American people," as if the offshoring of "American" jobs, the debt-enslavement of "American" college students, the real -estate-bubble Ponzi schemes, the commodification of healthcare, culture, and more or less every other aspect of society, not to mention the invasions and bombings of other countries, as if all this wasn't designed to serve the long-term interests of global Capitalism, and was simply the result of series of "mistakes" on the part of incompetent and misguided politicians.

The "failure" of the invasion and occupation of Iraq is a perfect example of this way of perceiving things. Yes, of course, for the "American people," it was, indeed, a colossal failure, a total waste of lives and money which accelerated the spread of terrorism both within the Middle East and around the world. However, for the transnational capitalist ruling classes, who couldn't care less about the American people, or the Iraqi people, or any other people, this "failure" was actually an enormous success, in terms of removing a major impediment to their eventual domination of the region, and upending the regional balance of power that had been established during the Cold War.

The invasion of Iraq, as you might remember, was planned well prior to September 2001. It was part of the agenda of the neo-conservative "Project for the New American Century," and deep -state players like Donald Rumsfeld, Paul Wolfowitz, Dick Cheney, Robert Kagan, and other corporatist think tank types. And of course it was … this was perfectly logical. After the USSR disintegrated, the Greater Middle East was ripe for restructuring — there was nothing to stop the military arm of global Capitalism (i.e., the US military) from moving in and beginning the process we've all been experiencing ever since.

Now, I'm not suggesting there's a bunch of capitalists sitting around in a room somewhere (e.g., at the annual Bilderberg Conference) consciously planning this kind of stuff. Conspiracy theories are fun and all that, but worldwide sociopolitical transformations (like the one we are in the middle of) are a bit more complex than a Hollywood movie, and probably have less to do with the intentions of individuals than we would like to think ... even extremely creepy individuals, like the ones whose names I just rattled off above.

What I am suggesting is that what we're experiencing, and have been experiencing since the end of the Cold War, is not a series of policy "blunders," but, rather, the emergence of a global power structure none of us really understands yet, not an empire in the classical sense, but an omnipresent power structure governed by the interests of global corporations, *not* by the interests of sovereign nations.[1]

It is in the interest of these corporations, and the global capitalist ruling classes (including government and deep-state elites), that we do not perceive the world this way, and that we continue to believe in the sovereignty of nations, and that we think of ourselves as citizens of these nations, despite all the evidence to the contrary.

Neo-Nationalism vs. Neoliberalism

The simulation of national sovereignty, in addition to acting as an ontological decoy, drawing our attention away from the fact that power is now primarily corporate, plays another essential role in the ongoing spread of global capitalism. As the global capitalist ruling classes seize control of more and more of the planet, absorbing what is left of actual society into their global simulation of society (i.e., a heterogeneously homogenous worldwide marketplace of products and services that no one really needs, the growth-obsessed production of which is destroying the entire biosphere) a considerable number of human beings are beginning to express their discontent.

In the US, the UK and Western Europe (i.e., the heartlands of the global capitalist empire), after nearly four decades of globalization, deregulation, privatization, austerity measures and debt-enslavement, the working classes have finally had enough of getting pissed on and being told it's raining ... or at least, according to mainstream media, the "less well-educated" members of them have.

This demeaning characterization is vitally important. The global capitalist ruling classes need to ensure that any resistance to globalization, privatization, and global neoliberalism, generally, is perceived

1 Bona fide scholars, which I am not, have been attempting to articulate this structure, which is more complex than I'm making it sound here, given how the corporate and government spheres overlap and feed each other, Antonio Negri, Michael Hardt, Noam Chomsky, Sam Gidin and Leo Panitch among them, each of whose books is probably worth reading, but you don't exactly need a PhD to perceive that corporations are running the show.

by the public as neo-nationalist, xenophobic, racist, or just plain ignorant. Not that a lot of it isn't. It is. A lot of it is, but not all of it is. The global capitalist ruling classes need us to believe that all of it is, and that the only two options available to us are neoliberalism and neo-nationalism.

The corporate media is working hard to convince us that these are our only alternatives. Their "coverage" of the Brexit referendum and its aftermath is a perfect example. Somehow, despite the doomsday campaign waged by the British liberal press, the UK voted to leave the EU, that bastion of European democracy, the one that is currently privatizing Greece in order to pay back the banks and speculators who made a killing lending billions to a country that everyone knew from day one was totally unfit for the single market, the one that is going to pass the TTIP, in some iteration, once they've cleaned it up.

According to the Oxbridge elites that dominate the British press, and their American counterparts across the pond, the only plausible explanation for the public's failure to follow orders, and respond to a series of last-minute threats issued by Obama, Soros and Junker, is a combination of neo-nationalism, xenophobia, and elderly dementia. The Guardian is reporting that an epidemic of British xenophobia has appeared out of thin air. Neo-nationalists, white supremacists, and other assorted racist twits, emboldened by their Brexit victory, are roving the streets in search of anyone "foreign-looking" to hurl abuse at.

Not that this isn't actually happening. It is, and not just in Britain either. The tide of neo-nationalist sentiment is on the rise throughout the Continent. Neo-nationalist parties have been making gains in Austria, Hungary, Sweden, Denmark, Finland, Greece, Switzerland, and elsewhere (not to mention the unabashed neo-Nazis Hillary Clinton's State Department helped to install in the new Ukrainian government, after they had regime-changed the old one). Here in Germany, the AfD (the "Alternatives for Germany" party), a pret-tied-up neo-nationalist front for uglier neo-Nazi types, while still fairly marginal, has been growing steadily. In France, it's Le Pen and the Front National. In the Netherlands, it's Geert Wilders — who, rumor has it, has kidnapped David Lynch's hairstylist — and the PVV (the "Party for Freedom").

Meanwhile, back in the USA, from what I've been able to gather from the pundits, Trump and his legions of down-market racists are still threatening the very fabric of democracy, never mind that, according to very same pundits, he has absolutely no chance of winning. Worse yet, it appears a troubling number of fanatical Bernie Sanders followers are refusing to get behind Hillary Clinton, who doesn't really need them anyway, as at this point she has the endorsement of every neoliberal and neoconservative pontificating talking head in existence, and is being sold by the liberal media as the thin blue line between "love" and "stability" and the thousand-year fascist Trumpian Reich.

But I don't want to make light of the threat. Neo-nationalist sentiment is definitely spreading, and white supremacists, neo-Nazis, and "alt-Right" creeps are making the most of it. The liberal press is churning out a non-stop series of "What-the-Hell-is-Happening-to-Democracy?" features, as if they didn't have the slightest clue. The Western intelligentsia, such as it is, appears to be completely baffled. Inexplicably, having been offered the chance to embrace a utopian capitalist future in which each and every one of us will be a thriving micro-entrepreneur marketing our asses to some global corporation, derivatives trader, or techno-oligarch, and all our outdated cultural values, religious beliefs, and personal prejudices, will either be eradicated or rendered meaningless interchangeable "lifestyle" choices and marketed back to us, a lot of people are retreating into the safety and familiarity of tribalism, as humans have done for millions of years. Yes, it's certainly quite a conundrum, all this neo-nationalist sentiment.

None of it, of course, if you believe the punditocracy, has anything to do with global capitalism, or the globalization of the labor market, or with the end of an historical era in which sovereign nations were actually sovereign, or with people's desire, however clouded by ignorance, to cling to some semblance of actual democracy, as opposed to being ruled by global corporations, investment banks, and their governmental proxies.

No, according to the corporate media, and to over-educated, half-bright, liberal authoritarians like Jonathan Rauch — for whom democracy is now an official disease worthy of inclusion in the next

DSM — the problem isn't global capitalism; the problem is people, and their "neurotic hatred" of politicians, and the whole "political class," who are simply trying to do the bidding of the global corporations that bought them. It isn't that the entire world is undergoing a radical restructuring (i.e., the transfer of sociopolitical power from sovereign nations to corporations, and the transformation of what remains of society into one big global capitalist marketplace), and that some of us aren't entirely thrilled. No, according to neoliberal sages like Rauch, Thomas Friedman, and numerous others, this "populist anger" is either some kind of mass behavioral syndrome or conduct disorder (e.g., "Oppositional Defiant Disorder" — think about that one for just a moment) or is symptomatic of pathological racism, xenophobia, "thought disorder," or some other psychological condition.

The Pathologization of Political Dissent

We can expect this type of pathologization of any and all resistance to capitalism to continue and accelerate throughout the future, as it functions as a perfect double bind. In a globally hegemonic system like ours, the system's ideology, no longer challenged by any credible competing ideology, transcends ideology and becomes normality. The enemy of the dominant class — and thus the one projected throughout the entire system as "everyone's enemy" — is no longer an external "foreign" enemy, but, rather, an internal, or "systemic" enemy. A deviation. An *abnormality*. The extremist, the terrorist, the neo-nationalist, the racist, the sociopathic child, cancer, depression, inappropriate anger, the malicious hacker, the government leaker … such are the threats to the new global order.

None of them poses a serious challenge to the hegemony of global capitalism (unless you believe that the corporate elites and the U.S. military are going to permit some Hitler-alike to undo everything they've been building for going on seventy years, in which case I've got a bridge to sell you). No, neo-nationalism and religious fundamentalism — short some sort of global catastrophe that wipes out modern civilization — are just vain attempts to turn back the clock to 17th Century despotism. (And as trendy as the Anonymous and Snowden stuff is, hacktivism and whistle-blowing pose no significant threat to power, no more than protesters masking up and throwing bottles at riot cops).

Neo-nationalism is a simulacrum … a living, breathing representation of something that has never "really" existed, other than as a simulacrum. Islamic fundamentalism, Christian fundamentalism, Stalinist communism, and every other attempt to reverse the spread of capitalism throughout the world since the 17th Century, also fall into this category.

Simulacra serve a vital purpose, namely, *to conceal the absence of something*. Religious icons and other representations of monotheistic deities do not conceal the existence of those deities; *they conceal the non-existence of those deities*.

Apologies for getting all Baudrillardian, but there isn't a better way to say this. Perhaps a more concrete example would be the "psychiatric disorder" I referred to above, Oppositional Defiant Disorder, which was first "discovered" in 1980. This "disorder" is, of course, a simulacrum (i.e., an invention of the psychiatric and pharmaceutical industries), but an actual disorder nonetheless, with categorizable symptoms, which respond to "treatment." All these new psychiatric "abnormalities," being simulacra, conceal the fact that *it is normality that does not exist* (and thus keep everyone obsessed with normality.)

The blood-dimmed tide of neo-nationalism currently sweeping the Western world is a simulacrum in this classical sense. It isn't a deceptive (i.e., "fake") alternative concealing an authentic (i.e., "real") alternative to the hegemony of global capitalism, but, rather, an all-too-real phenomenon concealing the fact that there is no alternative, and that, at present, an alternative is unimaginable (i.e., literally unimaginable, in that we are not yet capable of conceiving a credible alternative system, or any way to get there from here).

The global capitalist ruling classes are extremely fond of this simulacrum, as it distracts us from facing where we actually are, and from working together to conceive that alternative, or even just asking the kind of questions that might help us actually get there, someday.

It also keeps everyone terrified of terrorism, Islamic fundamentalism, neo-fascism, populism, Trumpism, and pretty much any other type of "extremism" they can think of, as if there were the slightest chance of any of these movements actually succeeding, and toppling global capitalism.

All right, that's enough reality for now. It's time to get back to the Internet. On behalf of the global capitalist ruling classes, and their partners in politics and the mainstream media, I apologize for this lengthy interruption, and return you to their regularly-programmed hysteria …

The Dawning of the Age of Non-Terrorist Terrorism

August 1, 2016

Of all the types of terrorist threats we are being conditioned to live in a more or less constant state of low-level fear of, the most terrifying of them all is the type we've witnessed throughout the Summer, a Summer so terrifying *The Guardian* is now officially calling it "The Summer of Fear."[1] Orlando, Nice, Würzberg, Munich, Reutlingen, Ansbach, Saint-Étienne-du-Rouvray ... the terror just keeps coming, and coming, like the monster in some blockbuster Hollywood movie. The most terrifying part of it is that these are no ordinary terrorist attacks carried out by ordinary terrorists at the behest of ordinary terrorist groups, but, rather, the work of a new breed of terrorist, a terrorist who has no connection whatsoever to any type of terrorist groups, is not primarily motivated by terrorism, and, basically, has nothing to do with terrorism.

Let's go ahead and call him the "non-terrorist terrorist."

According to the official narrative propagated by the corporate media, non-terrorist terrorism officially began in late September 2014 with a statement by Abu Muhammad al-Adnani, a terrorist spokesman for ISIS, ISIL, Daesh, or whatever we're calling it this week. This statement, which has since been quoted as often as humanly possible in the corporate press, exhorted decentralized terrorist cells, aspiring terrorists, and other random individuals, to launch attacks against innocent Westerners, to wit, to "[s]mash his head with a rock, or

---

1 *Connolly, Kate and Willsher, Kim, "Summer of fear: the anxious mood in Germany and France," The Guardian, 29 July, 2016*

slaughter him with a knife, or run him over with a car, or throw him down from a high place ..." and so on.

According to the same official narrative, the first known attack by a non-terrorist terrorist was carried out in Dijon, France (yes, the place the mustard comes from) in late December 2014, three months after the al-Adnani statement.[2] The prosecutor in the case described the perpetrator as a "barely coherent," mentally unbalanced, middle-aged man who used his car to mow down over a dozen pedestrians while shouting Islamic stuff out the window.

This, we are learning, is part of the cunning modus operandi of the non-terrorist terrorists, the way they are able to extensively plan and carry out terrifying terrorist attacks while posing as mentally disturbed individuals, or as sexually confused or alienated loners, who have absolutely nothing to do with terrorism.

This ruse was deployed again in Orlando, where the non-terrorist terrorist went as far as to pose as a closeted homosexual; and in Nice, where the attacker maintained his cover for years as a wife-beating petty criminal; and in Würzberg, where apparently the teenage terrorist had been masquerading as an orphaned refugee, but in fact was an insidious sleeper agent sent by ISIS to attack some random train in the middle of the German countryside.

According to knowledgeable terrorism experts, Western governments, and the mainstream media, we're going to be seeing more and more of these seemingly uncoordinated "terrorist" attacks, both on targets like Nice, which fit the narrative, but also on targets that make no sense, and that terrorists like ISIS have never even heard of, but to which they have nonetheless dispatched their agents to attack Asian tourists with kitchen knives and hatchets while shouting "Allahu Akbar" at the top of their lungs. Who knows where the next attack will take place? Vossevangen, Norway? Demming, New Mexico? Menomonie, Wisconsin? The Outer Hebrides? Your guess is as good as mine.

The point is, as the War on Terror (which, as you probably remember, President Obama officially ended in 2013) enters this new and more terrifying phase, we will need to prepare ourselves, both

---

2 The 2013 Boston Marathon bomb attack apparently doesn't count anymore, as it occurred before the al-Adnani statement, and thus doesn't fit the official narrative.

logistically and emotionally, for the dramatically heightened level of terror engendered by the non-terrorist terrorist threat, as well as the invasive "security measures" that will be required to pretend to combat it. Fear, as ever, will be the watchword. Everyone will need to do their part to assist the authorities in identifying, indefinitely detaining, and enhanced-interrogating potential non-terrorist terrorist suspects, and anyone else who looks kind of fishy.

Let's take a look at how that will work.

How to Spot a Non-Terrorist Terrorist

The non-terrorist terrorist is difficult to identify and place on a secret government watch-list, as he exhibits few (and sometimes none) of the characteristics of the conventional terrorist. Whereas the conventional terrorist is typically a devout Muslim, and a member of some notorious terrorist group, like ISIS, Al-Qaeda, or Al-Nusra Front (although the latter may not be terrorists, currently, depending on what's going on in Syria), the non-terrorist terrorist is usually not at all religious, is not a member of any terrorist group, and has absolutely no connection to terrorism.

This lack of any terrorist background, or any other ties to actual terrorism, given the current restrictive limits imposed on anti-Terror professionals by laws, national constitutions, and the like, effectively renders the non-terrorist terrorist undetainable in advance by government agents, anti-Terror police units, and corporate mercenaries, at least in developed Western countries, so they're going to need all the help they can get in terms of surveilling and profiling everyone. With that in mind, here are some tips for identifying potential non-terrorist terrorists.

The most important thing to remember is that the non-terrorist terrorist is definitely a Muslim, or at least is vaguely Muslim-looking, or has a Muslim-sounding name. White supremacists, neo-Nazis, heavily-armed fundamentalist Christians, and garden-variety white-skinned criminals, unattractive and dangerous though they may be, do not fall into the "terrorism" category, unless, that is, they blow up something like the Alfred P. Murrah Federal Building, but even that might not count anymore, as it happened before the War on Terror, and ... well, once you start calling white people "terrorists," the distinctions between things get really confusing.

In spite of the fact that he is definitely a Muslim, the non-terrorist terrorist exhibits any or all of a variety of "non-Muslim behaviors." He drinks, smokes, abuses drugs, is sexually promiscuous (or he aspires to promiscuity), does not attend mosque, rarely prays, and otherwise appears to be just another stressed-out, debt-burdened Western consumer trying to make sense of late-capitalist society, and to support himself (and, in some cases, his family) with some soul-crushing job at the foreign subsidiary of some global corporation he isn't even aware of, or as an Uber driver, or temporary security guard, or with some other type of micro-entrepreneurial activity that's making his life a living hell ... which feeds right into his other cover.

The non-terrorist terrorist often goes to great lengths to create the appearance of having had a long history of psychological and emotional problems. This cover (which the non-terrorist terrorist may begin constructing as early as his late-adolescence) may involve the feigning of a series of nervous breakdowns, or episodes of clinical depression, or suicide attempts, or other such symptoms.

Don't let this "emotionally unstable" act fool you by playing on your empathy for other human beings. If ever in doubt about a disturbed individual, or anyone expressing extremist views, or acting in any way unusual, it is best to just go ahead and report him, and let the authorities sort it out. You could be dealing with a non-terrorist terrorist in the process of "sudden self-radicalization."

The "Suddenly Self-Radicalized" Non-Terrorist Terrorist

Unlike the conventional (or "actual") terrorist, the non-terrorist terrorist is often radicalized shortly before the time of his attack, or during his attack, or shortly thereafter. "Radicalization" is a tricky process, which can occur in any number of ways, e.g., over time, in structured settings, but also in purely imaginary ways that only exist in the minds of the terrorists, or the minds of the media, or anti-terrorism experts. In any event, it's not like the old days, when aspiring terrorists were forced to attend those terrorist training camps out in the desert, and actually get involved with terrorism. Nowadays all it takes is the Internet, and sincere desire to radicalize yourself.

"Self-radicalization" is a growing problem, and not just among Islamic terrorists. "Radicalism" in any form that challenges global capitalism, neoliberalism, and other Western values, is spreading like a mass psychological disorder.[3] Like the child with Oppositional Defiant Disorder, sometimes even the non-terrorist terrorist (or whatever type of "self-radicalized" person) doesn't even realize he's becoming a terrorist, or a non-terrorist terrorist, until it's too late.

"Self-radicalization" often begins with irrational and inappropriate resentment, which is typically projected onto affluent individuals, corporations, investment banks, politicians, billionaires, members of the media, or the populations of other countries that happen to be invading or bombing the country of the "self-radicalizing" person in question. This misdirected pathological anger, if allowed to fester, inevitably leads to the thinking of extremist or terrorist thoughts, which leads to the tweeting of terrorist tweets, and to the posting of terrorist Facebook posts. In no time at all, the self-radicalizing person has transformed into a full-blown non-terrorist terrorist, and is snorting up lines of pulverized Captagon, drawing half-assed ISIS flags on the walls of his apartment with indelible markers, and loading up on weapons at Walmart, or whatever passes for Walmart in his country.

This is just a preliminary check-list of the hallmark features of the non-terrorist terrorist, which the mainstream media will be adding to as "The Summer of Fear" approaches its climax, and presumably throughout the indefinite future, as the Age of Non-Terrorist Terrorism continues, possibly until the end of Time.

A Word of Warning Regarding Terminology

All right, I know what you're probably thinking … you're thinking we've finally reached some level of absurdity with this calling people "terrorists" thing where the term completely loses its meaning, and its ability to scare the bejesus out of people.

---

3 Rauch, Jonathan, "How American Politics Went Insane," The Atlantic, July/August 2016 (in which Rauch diagnoses the American public's "pathological resentment of the political class.")

Fortunately, this is not at all the case. In fact, it's almost exactly the obverse — the more nonsensical, oxymoronic, and utterly meaningless the terms we use to describe the heinous, subhuman enemies (who want to slaughter us because of our freedom) are, the more meaningful, effective and terrifying they are. This is crucial when distinguishing between, for example, our friends in Saudi Arabia and barbarous mad-dog terrorists like ISIS, both of whom chop off people's heads for crimes like apostasy, idolatry, and adultery, but, of course, the Saudis are not savage terrorists, despite their involvement in the terrorist attacks of September 11, 2001, and … well, you can see the danger here, when you start to actually think about things.

The point is, our new "non-terrorist terrorist" designation should not confuse or call into question the widely-acknowledged definition (and constant repetition) of the terms "terrorist," "terror," and "terrorism," whether of the "non-terrorist" or "terrorist" type. Terrorism is not a word game, or some specious semiotic construct, or an essentially arbitrary made-up label that can be slapped onto any type of violent activity or ideology we want to demonize.

Terrorism is terrorism. The word means exactly what it means, whatever that might possibly be at this point. You can look it up on the Internet, on Google, or Wikipedia, or whatever.

And as for the "non-terrorist terrorist" designation, let's not get all freaked out about it and make it any more confusing than it is. We can sit around and argue forever over whether the "non-terrorist terrorist" is a "terrorist," but, honestly, where is that going to get us? The simple fact of the matter is, as the adjectival in the term denotes, the non-terrorist terrorist is not a terrorist … nevertheless he is a terrorist, and the fact that he is and is not a terrorist simultaneously defines what he is and makes absolutely no difference at all, at least not within the official narrative.

No, despite what terrorist apologists will tell you, designating some terrorists "non-terrorist terrorists" doesn't mean they aren't terrorists, or that there isn't any such thing as "terrorism," except within the simulation of "reality" the global capitalist ruling classes need to maintain to keep the masses entertained and borderline paranoid, as they (i.e., the capitalists, not the masses) transform the rest of the entire planet into a combination shopping mall/labor camp.

If that were true ... well, the War on Terror would be nothing but an elaborate farce, a simulacrum that was there to distract us from the sociopolitical and economic dynamics of the historical period we were actually living through … which dynamics might have something to do with something a bit more complex than "terror," "evil," "hate," and other empty but terror-inspiring words like that.

As stressful as things are at the moment, imagine how exhausting that would be, having to think about all that stuff, transnational capitalism's ideology, the manufacturing of consensus reality, all the childish narratives we would be being fed moment by moment by the corporate-owned media, and the amount of mental energy it would take to try to resist it on a daily basis … but then, seeing as you've made it to the end of this essay, I'm pretty sure you already have.

The Rise and Fall of the Trumpian Reich

September 21, 2016

So, here it is, mid-September, and it looks like Trump is still in this thing. Which is pretty amazing when you think about it. Despite the Hitlerization of this clown by more or less every major organ of the mainstream media throughout the spring, and his Russification throughout the summer, and his racism, narcissism, and blatant idiocy, he's polling within a couple points of Clinton.

This was not supposed to happen. Neoliberal elites are panicking. It's not that they're worried about Trump himself as much as this "populist backlash" thing, which appears to be spreading throughout the West, and is screwing with stuff like the TPP, the European Union, and Great Britain, and so on. Which means, from now until November 8, the liberal media will be deploying every emotionally manipulative weapon in their arsenal to guilt-trip you into voting for Clinton, as if democracy and life itself depended on it.

Here are some examples from the weekend papers …

The New York Times, having already done the "Trump-is-Hitler" thing to death, broke out the Klu Klux Klan analogy, proclaiming Trump "the Grand Wizard of Birtherism."[1] *The Guardian* reported that he called on his brownshirts to assassinate Clinton at a rally in Miami.[2] *The Washington Post*, after conducting an in-depth analysis of three or four of Trump's tweets, agreed that he was raising "the specter of violence."[3] And, following Jimmy Fallon's hair-mussing incident, *Slate* announced that from this point on "there is no longer

1 Blow, Charles M., "Trump, Grand Wizard of Birtherism," The New York Times, September 17, 2016

2 Luscombe, Richard, "Donald Trump: Clinton's bodyguards should disarm and see what happens," The Guardian, September 17, 2016

3 Blake, Aaron, "Donald Trump just made his most direct comment yet about violence against Hillary Clinton," The Washington Post, September 17, 2016

a non-partisan space … there are no Switzerlands in the 2016 election."[4] You're either with Clinton or you're a Hitler-lover.

The problem is, it isn't working (or it isn't working well enough), the tried and true Hitlerization tactic. Perhaps it's the fact that Trump is an American. Hitlerization works much better on foreign "Hitlers," like Ho Chi Min, Noriega, Milošević, or Saddam Hussein. Or maybe they've just used it too often. I mean, sure, you can trick folks into believing that someone is a "modern day Hitler" six, maybe seven times running, but eventually they start to feel like suckers who keep falling for the same crap over and over. Norman Solomon wrote a book about this, back in 2005, I believe.[5] But whatever, this is no time for history or critical thinking. There's too much at stake.

With that in mind, as a loyal American, I feel it's time to dispense with satire and contribute to the effort to help the Democrats, and the Clintons, and their friends at Goldman Sachs, and the entire transnational capitalist ruling class, save the world from the coming Trumpocalypse. I intend to do that by scaring you shitless, because I can't really think of any other reason you would want to buy into this mockery of democracy and actually go out vote for Clinton … and, apparently, neither can she or her people, because the fear thing seems to be all they've got. So no more pussyfooting around. Here it is, the nightmare scenario. Vote for Clinton, or this is what you get.

Friday, January 20, 2017

Immediately after being sworn in as President, so right there on the Capitol steps, as a horrified nation watches on TV, Trump declares a National State of Emergency "to deal with the illegal immigrant threat," dissolves the U.S. Congress, suspends the Constitution, and appoints himself "Leader of the Western World." He orders the military to assemble its troops in football stadiums with corporate names and swear an oath of allegiance to him personally. He orders NORAD to go to DEFCON 3, for reasons he refuses to clarify. Global markets plunge precipitously. The entire American deep-

4 Paskin, Willa, "Jimmy Fallon Mussing Donald Trump's Hair Is the Point of No Return," Slate, September 16, 2016

5 Solomon, Norman, War Made Easy, Wiley, June 1, 2005

state nexus (i.e., DOD, DHS, NSA, CIA, DOJ, NSC, CFR, Wall Street, et al.) have no choice but to follow his orders, because they have to respect the election results. In spite of the fact that Trump clearly intends to strip them of their enormous power, and establish some sort of megalomaniacal fascist empire and take over the world, they surrender, and do whatever he says.

Saturday, January 21

Trump appoints David Duke both Director of the Department Homeland Security and Chief of Staff. Duke promptly orders the DHS logo to be revised to prominently feature "Pepe the Frog." Meanwhile, the Clintons, and most of the Democratic Party leadership, are arrested by Trump's personal "Security Forces," charged with sedition, and spirited away to an undisclosed location. Trump closes the United Nations headquarters in New York, nationalizes the Wall Street banks, unilaterally abrogates every international trade deal the U.S. has ever signed on to, and orders "persons of un-American ethnicity" to report to their local DHS office for "processing." Again, nobody is able to stop him, because "he won the election fair and square."

Sunday, January 22

By Sunday morning, the highly spirited but strictly non-violent anti-Trump protests that erupted overnight around the country have been brutally crushed by the U.S. military, which just mindlessly follows the obviously insane orders of recently unretired General Michael T. Flynn, Trump's Chairman of the Joint Chiefs of Staff. Wisps of smoke rise from the National Mall, where David Duke and his DHS stormtroopers, most of them in full Ku Klux Klan regalia, conducted some sort of mass cross burning during the night. Trump nationalizes the television networks. He nationalizes the Internet and names Kellyanne Conway "Internet Czarina." He closes the airports and seals the borders. The global economy completely collapses. Hoarding, rioting, and looting are rampant. The entire world is powerless to stop this, because, after all, "he won the election." The global capitalist ruling classes tremble in fear in their yachts and mansions, wishing they weren't bound by "the rules" to respect the people's choice this one time.

Monday, January 23

America wakes to finds its streets occupied by Russian soldiers, most of whom are clearly drunk. Trump and Putin appear together on the lawn of the White House, both of them shirtless, looking like they've been up all night, and announce a new bilateral arrangement whereby the two of them will rule the world "with iron fists of decisive greatness." The Russian invasion is only temporary. They all fly home at the end of the day, and immediately invade the European Union, for reasons that make no sense to anyone. India and Pakistan nuke each other. NORAD goes to DEFCON 2.

Tuesday, January 24

The Anschluss of Mexico and Canada begins ... and ends victoriously three hours later. Trump, out of "an abundance of caution," goes ahead and takes Central America, and orders a wall built on the Colombian border. Europe, at this point, has been reduced to rubble. Brussels and Berlin have been tactically nuked, rumor has it by Nigel Farage, who has somehow assumed control of Great Britain. Marine le Pen, who is running France, has been frantically trying to get through to Trump and find out who to surrender to, but unfortunately all the hotlines are down. Meanwhile, back in the USA, David Duke, and a handful of other racist losers you've never heard of, have gathered in a villa on the shores of Lake Pontchartrain to sketch out "a solution to the Mexican problem." Israel, figuring "oh, what the hell," goes ahead and nukes Iran. Putin, relaxing in his Black Sea dacha with a bevy of bimbos and Edward Snowden, watches it all unfold on TV, laughing demonically as democracy burns. Nobel Prize-winning economist Paul Krugman, who has somehow miraculously survived thus far, emerges from hiding to scold millennials for stubbornly refusing to vote for Clinton, the only person who could have prevented all this.

Wednesday, January 25

China nukes Russia. Russia nukes Japan. The U.K. nukes Brussels, which has already been nuked. Israel nukes Iran and Egypt. North Korea nukes South Korea. France, apparently, nukes itself. Trump, consummate showman to the end, stages a enormous Riefenstahlian rally in honor of Wotan in Central Park, proclaims himself "the one-eyed God," and orders all Americans to poison themselves with a mixture of cyanide and Peach Mango Kool-Aid, the trademark for which he has recently acquired with a loan from some no-name bank he nationalized, all of which could have been avoided if people had just shut up and voted for Clinton.

Thursday, January 26

The Trumpocalypse. The end of life on Earth. This is humanity's final punishment for ignoring the warnings of neoliberal pundits and refusing to vote for Hillary Clinton. Trump, sensing the end is nigh, and (like every other megalomaniac) wanting to take all of Creation with him, launches his remaining nukes at Putin. He does this from the open bomb bay of a Northrop Grumman B-2 Spirit. As Putin launches his retaliatory strike, cursing the soul of his former puppet, Trump rides the snow white B83 thermonuclear gravity ordnance, Slim Pickens-style, down out of the heavens, wearing a "Make America Great" cap to keep his hair from looking silly …

Shantih … shantih … shantih.

The Pathologization of Dissent

October 27, 2016

According to the liberal mainstream media, in a recent speech in West Palm Beach, Donald Trump finally completely lost it. Sawing the air with his tiny hands in a unmistakeably Hitlerian manner, he spat out a series of undeniably hateful anti-Semitic code words ... like "political establishment," "global elites" and, yes, "international banks." He even went so far as to claim that "corporations" and their (ahem) "lobbyists" have millions of dollars at stake in this election, and are trying to pass the TTP, not to benefit the American people, but simply to enrich themselves. He then went on to accuse the media of collaborating with "the Clinton machine," presumably to benefit these "global elites" and "international banks" and "lobbyists."

Now, a lot of folks didn't immediately recognize the secret meanings of these fascist code words, and mistakenly assumed that "global elites" referred to the transnational capitalist ruling classes, and that "lobbyists" referred to actual lobbyists, and that "banks" meant ... well ... you know, banks.

As it turned out, this was completely wrong. None of these words actually meant what they meant, not in anti-Semitic CodeSpeak. So the mainstream media translated for us. "Political establishment" meant "the Jews." "Global elites" also meant "the Jews." "Banks" meant "Jews." "Lobbyists" meant "Jews." Even "corporate media" meant "Jews." Apparently, Trump's entire speech was a series of secret dog-whistle signals to his legions of neo-Nazi goons, who, immediately following Clinton's victory, are going to storm out of their hidey holes, frontally attack the US military, overthrow the U.S. government, and, yes, you guessed it ... "kill the Jews."

OK, maybe I'm exaggerating the mainstream media's reaction just a little bit. Or maybe Trump's speech really was that fascistic. Judge for yourself. Read the transcript.[1] Then compare the reactions of *The Wall Street Journal*,[2] *The New York Times*,[3] *The Washington Post*,[4] *The Inquirer*,[5] *The Guardian*,[6] and other leading broadsheets, and magazines and blogs like *Mother Jones*,[7] *Forward*,[8] *Slate*,[9] and a host of others, most of which rely on Jonathan Greenblatt, CEO of the Anti-Defamation League and former Special Assistant to the President, as their authoritative source on Trumpian cryptology. (Greenblatt, incidentally, should know better, given the treatment he has received from hard-line Zionist publications for refusing to demonize Black Lives Matter, and for "taking sides against" the State of Israel.)

Look, I'm not defending Donald Trump, who I consider a self-aggrandizing idiot and a soulless huckster of the lowest order, and whose supporters include a lot of real anti-Semites, and racists, and misogynists, and other such creeps. I'm simply trying to point out how the corporate media have, for months, been playing the same hysterical tune like an enormous Goebbelsian keyboard instrument, and how millions of Americans are singing along (as they were before the invasion of Iraq), and how terribly disturbing that is.

In case you didn't instantly recognize it, the name of the tune is "This guy is Hitler!" and it isn't the short vulgarian fingers of Donald Trump that are tickling the ivories. And no, it isn't "the Jews" either. It's the corporate media, and the corporations that own them, and the rest of the global capitalist ruling classes … in other words, those

---

1 "Transcript: Donald Trump's Speech Responding To Assault Accusations," National Public Radio, October 13, 2016 (https://www.npr.org/2016/10/13/497857068/transcript-donald-trumps-speech-responding-to-assault-accusations)

2 Stephens, Brett, "The Plot Against America," Wall Street Journal, October 17, 2016

3 Chokshi, Niraj, "Trump Accuses Clinton of Guiding Global Elite Against U.S. Working Class," The New York Times, October 13, 2016

4 Rucker, Philip and Sullivan, Shawn, "Trump says groping allegations are part of a global conspiracy to help Clinton," The Washington Post, October 13, 2016

5 Rubin, Trudy, "Trump goes deeper into dangerous waters," The Inquirer, October 16, 2016

6 Bixby, Scott, Phipps, Claire, and McCarthy, Tom, "Donald Trump says sexual misconduct accusers are 'horrible, horrible liars' – as it happened," The Guardian, October 14, 2016

7 Rosenthal, Max J., "Trump Escalates Attacks on His Accusers, Denigrating Their Looks," Mother Jones, October 14, 2016

8 Guttman, Nathan, "At Florida Rally, Trump Evokes Specter of 'International Banks' and Jews Cheer, Too," Forward, October 13, 2016

9 Saletan, William, "Springtime for Donald," Slate, October 14, 2016

"global elites."

The thing I find particularly disturbing is how these rather mundane observations — i.e., (a) that a global ruling class exists, (b) that it is primarily corporate in character, and (c) that this class is pursuing its own interests and not the interests of sovereign states — how such observations are being stigmatized as the ravings of unhinged anti-Semites. This stigmatization is not limited to Trumpists. Anyone to the left of Clinton is now, apparently, an anti-Semite. For example, Roger Cohen, in *The New York Times*, riding the tsunami of condemnation of the insidious verbiage of Trump's West Palm speech, executed an extended smear-job on Jeremy Corbyn and his "Corbynistas" (they're fond of coining these epithets, the media), denouncing their virulent "anti-Americanism," "anti-capitalism," "anti-globalism," and "anti-Semitic anti-Zionism."[10]

Which ... OK, let me hasten to add, and stress, and underscore, and repeatedly emphasize, is not to imply that the U.K. Labour Party, or the British Left, or the American Left, or any other Left, is anti-Semitism-free. Of course not. There are anti-Semites everywhere. That isn't the point. Or it isn't my point.

My point is that this stigmatization campaign is part of a much larger ideological project ... one that has little to do with Trump, or Jeremy Corbyn, and their respective parties. Smearing one's political opponents is nothing new, of course, it's as old as the hills. But what we're witnessing is more than smears.

As I proposed in these pages back in July,[11] political dissent is being gradually pathologized (i.e., stigmatized as aberrant or "abnormal" behavior, as opposed to a position meriting discussion). Consider the abnormalization of Sanders, back when he was talking about "banks," "global elites," and other things that matter, or the media's portrayal of British voters as racists in the wake of the Brexit referendum. And, yes, the charges being leveled against Trump, much as we might despise the man. Anti-Semitism, inciting violence, paranoid conspiracy theorizing, insurrection, treason, et cetera — these are not legitimate arguments one needs to counter with superior arguments; they are symptoms of deviations from a norm, signs of criminality or

10 Cohen, Roger, "Anti-Semitic Anti-Zionism," The New York Times, October 18, 2016

11 The pages of CounterPunch and the Consent Factory blog..

pathology, which is increasingly how the corporate ruling classes are dismissing anyone who attempts to challenge them.

A line is being drawn in the ideological sand. On one side of it are the decent people, the "normal" people, in their business wear, with their university degrees, and prescriptions, and debts. On the other side are … well, the "deplorables," the ignorant, racist, anti-Semitic, neo-nationalist, populist extremists. This line cuts through both the Left and the Right (supersedes both Left and Right), making bedfellows of supposed adversaries like Obama, Clinton, Kagan, Wolfowitz, Scowcroft, and their ilk on the Normal team, and a motley crew of Trumpists, Putinists, European populists, Corbynistas, Sandernistas, socialists, anarchists, Wikileakers, anti-Zionists, anti-capitalists, neo-Nazis, Black Lives Matterers, angry Greek pensioners, environmental activists, religious zealots, the Ku Klux Klan, David Graeber, most of the contributors to CounterPunch, and various other "extremist" types (many of whom detest each other), in the Deplorables' current starting line-up.

The corporate media is sending a message … a message aimed at a much broader audience than undecided American voters (assuming such creatures really exist). The message is, "get with the fucking program, or get stigmatized as an anti-Semite, or a racist, or a Russian spy, or whatever." The message is, "drop the populist rhetoric, shut the hell up about the Wall Street banks, and the corporations, and the 'one percent,' and … actually … forget about politics completely, except for identity politics, of course. Go ahead and knock yourself out with that." The message is, "you're either with us or against us … and it doesn't matter why you're against us, or what it is you think you're for. Right, Left … who gives a shit? It's one big Basket of Deplorables to us."

This message, of course, displays all of the hallmarks of the classic authoritarian mentality, the need for nearly total conformity, mindless allegiance to one's so-called superiors, delegitimization of all opposing viewpoints, and the infantile type of hero-worship figures like Obama and Clinton inspire … not the old-fashioned authoritarianism that would-be despots like Trump represent, but, rather, a more attractive version, a hopey, changey, lovey version, where there are no frightening Hitlerian leaders barking out anti-Semitic code words, and no one is exterminating thousands of people in faraway countries they want to destabilize in order to entirely dominate the region. No, this is the version where Obama sells the TPP on the Jimmy Fallon show, and wars of aggression are not wars of aggression, but "humanitarian interventions." It's also the version where universal healthcare is, regrettably, "unrealistic," but $38 billion for the State of Israel so it can operate its apartheid state, and weapons sales to Saudi Arabia, so they can bomb the shit out of farmers in Yemen, and cut off people's heads for blasphemy, is somehow in "America's vital interests."

But what do I know? I'm just a satirist. I should probably leave all this complex stuff, like what is and isn't in my interest, and what words actually mean and all that, to the experts in the mainstream media. Since they did so well decoding Trump's speech, maybe they could translate some of these other code words I've been having trouble with, like the ones I put in scare quotes above, or other such code words, like "enemy combatant," "free trade agreement," "security barrier," "indefinite detention," "targeted killing," or "troubled asset relief program."

I could go on, but I probably shouldn't. Odds are, I'm already on the list of Putin-worshiping, anti-Semitic, racist, misogynist, neo-nationalist, non-standing up for the National Anthem, conspiracy-theorizing America-haters. The last thing I need to do at this point is start jabbering about how the United States is an authoritarian corporatist dystopia ruled by a global capitalist elite that couldn't give less of a shit about Americans (or any other actual people living in any other actual countries), where the corporate media can whip up mass fanatical support for wars of aggression, or corporate puppets, by pointing their fingers at yet another bogeyman and shouting "Hitler" at the top of their lungs. Next thing you know I'd be writing about "banks," and "global corporations," and "national sovereignty," and we all know what that's about, don't we?

Trumpocalypse

November 25, 2016

So, it looks like we've got about fifty-five days until the end of Western civilization, and possibly even life on Earth. That's right, the Trumpocalypse has officially begun. According to the torrent of histrionic tirades the liberal corporate media have been projectile vomiting out at us since November 9, we are on the brink of a new "Age of Darkness."[1] "Globalization is dead; white supremacy has triumphed!"[2] America is descending into "racial Orwellianism,"[3] or Zionist anti-Semitism,[4] or "a bottomless pit of Fascism,"[5] or something.

In any event, in less than two months, the American ruling classes will peacefully surrender their control of the government to Donald J. Trump, and his legions of fanatical "Alt-Right" fascists, because Hillary Clinton lost an election ... or so goes the hard-line liberal narrative.

According to this narrative, shortly after Trump's inauguration on January 20, the United States military (which presumably has just been waiting for an opportunity to mindlessly follow some dictator's orders) will begin the round-up of all non-white Americans, and LGBTQ persons, and women, and journalists, and start loading them onto the trains, and so on. The American ruling classes, despite the fact that they control the legislature, the banks, the media, and the military-industrial complex, will have no choice but to allow this to happen ... because, after all, Trump won fair and square.

---

1 Freedland, Jonathan, "If Donald Trump wins, it'll be a new age of darkness," The Guardian, November 4, 2016

2 Mason, Paul, "Globalisation is dead, and white supremacy has triumphed," The Guardian, November 9, 2016

3 Blow, Charles M., "Trump: Making America White Again," The New York Times, November 21, 2016

4 Gjeltin, Tom, "Could A Trump Presidency Be Pro-Israel And White Nationalist At The Same Time?" National Public Radio, Morning Edition, November 21, 2016

5 Olberman, Keith, "Should We Give Donald Trump a Chance?" The Resistance with Keith Olberman, GQ, November 16, 2016

This scenario will also unfold in Europe. Front National, AfD, UKIP, Golden Dawn in Greece, and other such neo-nationalist parties will band together with the Trumpian Reich and establish some sort of international neo-nationalist New World Order, which will form an alliance with Vladimir Putin, and Iran (and any other demons you can think of), and set about destroying the interdependent, supranational neoliberal economy that the global capitalist ruling classes have been implementing over the last seventy years. No one will be able to prevent this. The utterly remorseless corporate leaders of the most powerful global-hegemonic system in human history will sit idly by as nation after nation falls to the forces of the "Alt-Right" revolution.

Seriously, this is the level of discourse the corporate media are churning out, and that is being recycled on social networks. Shameless mandarins of the corporatist Left like Krugman,[6] Friedman,[7] Jamelle Bouie,[8] Jonathan Chait,[9] David Corn,[10] Kurt Eichenwald (who appears to have completely lost it and started stalking Susan Sarandon on Twitter), and their counterparts across the Atlantic, are assuring us it's pretty much the end of the world, which is what we deserve for not voting for Clinton. Liberal parents are terrorizing their children with visions of the approaching holocaust.[11] The "national gathering" of 275 fascist creeps in a D.C. restaurant is now, apparently, front page news.[12] This tiny group of neo-Nazi asshats (who practically no one had ever heard of before the mainstream media showered them with coverage, although they've been around for years) is purportedly just the tip of the enormous "Alt-Right" iceberg now menacing America.

---

6 *Bryan, Bob, "Krugman: It's looking more and more like the election was swung by the FBI in virtual 'alliance with Putin'," Business Insider, November 17, 2016*

7 *Schwartz, Ian, "Thomas Friedman: Trump Presidency A 'Moral 9/11'," Real Clear Politics, November 12, 2016*

8 *Bouie, Jamelle, "There's No Such Thing as a Good Trump Voter," Slate, November 15, 2016*

9 *Chait, Jonathan, "Forget Canada. Stay and Fight for American Democracy," November 9, 2016*

10 *Corn, David, "The NSA Chief Says Russia Hacked the 2016 Election. Congress Must Investigate," Mother Jones, November 16, 2016*

11 *Sorkin, Aaron, "A moving letter written to Sorkin's 15-year-old daughter Roxy and her mother Julia Sorkin following Trump's election win," Vanity Fair, November 9, 2016*

12 *Hendrix, Steve and Cox, John Woodrow, "After Trump victory, attendance rises at annual white nationalist conference in D.C.," The Washington Post, November 19, 2016*

The good news is, the "Resistance" is back. Militant liberals are out in the streets battling fascism with pithy placards, in a peaceful, non-violent fashion, of course. A Safety Pin Brigade has been hastily organized, and has set out to accessorize fascism to death. Owen Jones is flying in from London to lead the anti-Trumpian uprising. His colleague at *The Guardian*, Steven Thrasher, is heading up the "abnormalization" effort.[13] And, of course, *The Nation* magazine will be hosting a luxury Caribbean cruise for affluent anti-fascist liberals (spa, paddle tennis, and yoga included.)

These liberals, of course, are the very same liberals who have had no problems whatsoever with the bombing of seven Muslim countries, the refusal to prosecute the Bush regime's war crimes, the arbitrary assassination of anyone the President feels like assassinating, and other such hopey changey features of the Obama regime for the past eight years. They have also not been terribly troubled by the knowledge that most of the products they purchase are being manufactured by de facto slaves in "developing countries" the corporations they're invested in have been privatizing, or by their racially-segregated neighborhoods and schools ... which, of course, they have nothing to do with, personally. But whatever, at least they're out there now, defending us all from the Forces of Darkness, or at least the simulation thereof.

Which is not to deny the rising tide of neo-nationalism throughout the West, or the xenophobia that is part and parcel of it, or that Trump is feeding off that sentiment, as are other neo-nationalist parties. This neo-nationalist backlash, however, is no real threat to neoliberalism, at least not over the longer term. And, make no mistake, it is neoliberalism that the liberal Left is staunchly defending. While I hate to disagree with Cornel West, what we are experiencing is not the death of neoliberalism,[14] but, rather, the death throes of national sovereignty.

Neoliberalism, let's remember, is just a new name for laissez-faire capitalism, which has been evolving out of feudal despotism since

13 Thrasher, Steven W., "Don't let Donald Trump become the new normal," The Guardian, November 14, 2016

14 West, Cornel, "Goodbye, American neoliberalism. A new era is here," The Guardian, November 17, 2016

some point in the 16th Century. The sovereign nation-state, which capitalism needed, first, to replace the feudal aristocracies, then, to advance us to where we are now (i.e., a global-hegemonic economic system policed by a single super-nation-state), has become a liability to capitalism. Though it continues to need the nation-state as an administrative/military apparatus, the sovereignty aspect has outlived its usefulness. It did this circa 1990, when global corporations gained unfettered access to a worldwide labor market they could ruthlessly exploit.

And now these globalized corporations, and the investment banks that trade their stock, and the politicians whose campaigns they fund, are going to allow the Trump regime to bring American jobs back home, and crash the entire global economy?

Call me crazy, but that seems unlikely.

The neo-nationalist backlash we're witnessing is not some inexplicable outbreak of xenophobic hatred and racism; it's a reaction to the loss of national sovereignty. Despite what the corporate media will tell you, people aren't total idiots. They realize that power is shifting from national governments to global corporations, and they're none too pleased about this development. The neo-nationalists (who are also not idiots) are capitalizing on this extreme displeasure. Some of these neo-nationalists are fascists, or "ethno-nationalists," and some are not. It doesn't actually make much difference, as the problem for the neo-nationalists is, their national economies are already globalized, as are their national financial systems. They can wave the flag as much as they like, but there isn't any going back at this point, not without committing national suicide.

Take the United States for example. Imagine what would happen to Apple's balance sheets (or what consumers would have to pay for their iPhones) if the company were forced to give up its slave labor. The same is true for most corporations, and most of the consumer products we own. Greece is another example, of course. They called a national referendum, and the people voted to reject the terms that the Troika was ramming down their throats, so the government simply ignored the people, because what were they going to do, after all, start a violent revolution? That's what all the militarized cops are for. The Brexit process will also be interesting, assuming it ever actually happens and that the Brits don't call a second referendum to nullify the results of the first. I could go on, but I don't think I have to ... no, I'm going to go out on a limb here and predict that neoliberalism will somehow survive the horrors of the Trumpian Rcich.

As for those horrors, all hysteria aside, odds are, they're going to be fairly horrible. And I don't just mean swastikas painted on storefronts. Steve Bannon, the Trump regime's Chief Strategist, unlike Trump, is not a babbling imbecile. He appears to be an extremely intelligent, long-term thinking, staunchly Zionist, "Judeo-Christian values" zealot, who is looking forward to a War Against Islam, which shouldn't be too hard to sell to Americans, considering that the USA has been bombing, invading and otherwise attacking the Middle East since the end of the Cold War, with the support of liberals and conservatives alike. This War Against Islam will dovetail nicely with the global capitalist ruling classes' broader objectives in the Middle East (namely, to destabilize and restructure the region, which they've been aggressively doing since the 1990s).

ISIS will be more than happy to cooperate, as they are also looking forward to this war. General Flynn will be ecstatic, as will Lockheed Martin, General Dynamics, Raytheon, Boeing, Northrop Grumman, and assorted other merchants of death. One or two serious terrorist attacks should be enough to get the ball rolling. An Osama bin Laden-caliber bogeyman, while not a requirement, would certainly help to reunite our divided country. Just think back to the weeks and months in the wake of the September 11 attacks, how America came together as a nation .... as they say in the motion picture business, the story pretty much writes itself.

Manufacturing Normality

December 6, 2016

Sometime circa mid-November, in the wake of Hillary Clinton's defeat (i.e., the beginning of the end of democracy), the self-appointed Guardians of Reality, better known as the corporate media, launched a worldwide marketing campaign against the evil and perfidious scourge of "fake news." This campaign is now at a fever pitch. Media outlets throughout the empire are pumping out daily dire warnings of the imminent, existential threat to our freedom posed by the "fake news" menace. This isn't the just the dissemination of disinformation, propaganda, and so on, that's been going on for thousands of years ... Truth itself is under attack. The very foundations of Reality are shaking.

Who's behind this "fake news" menace? Well, Putin, naturally, but not just Putin. It appears to be the work of a vast conspiracy of virulent anti-establishment types, ultra-alt-rightists, ultra-leftists, libertarian retirees, armchair socialists, Sandernistas, Corbynistas, ontological terrorists, fascism normalizers, anti-globalization freaks, and just garden variety Clinton-haters.

Fortunately, for us, the corporate media is hot on the trail of this motley of scoundrels. As you're probably aware, *The Washington Post* recently published a breathtaking piece of Pulitzer-quality investigative journalism shamelessly smearing hundreds of alternative publications (like the one you're reading[1]) as "peddlers of Russian propaganda." The piece, a classic McCarthyite smear job perpetrated by the *Post*'s Craig Timberg,[2] was based on the groundless, paranoid claims of what Timberg unironically describes as "two teams of independent researchers," The Foreign Policy Research Institute,

1 This essay first appeared in CounterPunch.

2 Timberg, Craig, "Russian propaganda effort helped spread fake news during election, experts say," The Washington Post, November 24, 2016

a third-rate, former anti-communist think tank, and an anonymous website, propornot.com, that no one had ever heard of prior to its sudden appearance on the Internet last August, and which, based on the tenor of its tweets and emails, appears to be run by Beavis and Butthead.

The Washington Post has been catching some flak for taking this courageous "pro-truth" stand against the forces of Putinist falsehood and fakery. A host of dangerously extremist publications, like *CounterPunch*,[3] *The Intercept*,[4] *Rolling Stone*,[5] *The Nation*,[6] *The New Yorker*,[7] *Fortune Magazine*,[8] and *US News & World Report*,[9] have lambasted *The Post* for its "shoddy," "lazy," or otherwise sub-par journalism practices.

The Post, of course, is "backing its boy," and refusing to apologize for defending democracy, as it has throughout its storied history, like when it smeared Gary Webb as retribution for reporting the CIA-Contra connection, more or less destroying his career as a journalist,[10] or when it blatantly shilled for Hillary Clinton throughout her ugly, fear-mongering campaign, notably publishing sixteen negative pieces on Sanders in sixteen hours,[11] or when it ran a story on how Clinton might have been poisoned by secret Putinist agents[12] ... and these are just a few of the highlights.

But I don't want to single out T*he Washington Post*, or its Executive

---

3 Frank, Joshua, "CounterPunch as Russian Propagandists: The Washington Post's Shallow Smear," CounterPunch, December 2, 2016

4 Greenwald, Glenn, "Washington Post Disgracefully Promotes a McCarthyite Blacklist From a New, Hidden, and Very Shady Group," The Intercept, November 26, 2016

5 Taibbi, Matt, "The 'Washington Post' 'Blacklist' Story Is Shameful and Disgusting," Rolling Stone, November 28, 2016

6 Carden, James, "The Washington Post Promotes a McCarthyite Blacklist," The Nation, November 28, 2016

7 Chen, Adrian, "The Propaganda About Russian Propaganda," The New Yorker, December 1, 2016

8 Ingram, Matthew, "No, Russian Agents Are Not Behind Every Piece of Fake News You See," Fortune, November 25, 2016

9 Nelson, Steven, "Publications Called Russian-Propaganda Distributors Consider Suing Anonymous 'Experts'," U.S. News & World Report, November 29, 2016

10 Cockburn, Alex, "Why They Hated Gary Webb," CounterPunch, December 18, 2004

11 Johnson, Adam, "Washington Post Ran 16 Negative Stories on Bernie Sanders in 16 Hours," Fairness & Accuracy in Reporting, March 8, 2016

12 Boren, Cindy, "The Man Who Discovered CTE Thinks Hillary Clinton Might Have Been Poisoned," The Washington Post, September 12, 2016

Editor, Marty Baron, who is clearly a paragon of journalistic ethics. The rest of the corporate media have also been mercilessly flogging the "fake news" hysteria, and the "Putinist propaganda" hysteria, and the "normalizing of fascism" hysteria, and beating the "post-truth" drum to death. *The Guardian*, *The New York Times*, et al., NPR, the TV news networks, the entire mainstream media chorus is barking out the message in perfect synch.

So what is really going on here?

As I suggested in these pages previously,[13] what we're experiencing is the pathologization, or the abnormalization, of political dissent (i.e., the systematic stigmatization of any and all forms of non-compliance with neoliberal consensus reality). Political distinctions like "left" and "right" are disappearing, and are being replaced by imponderable distinctions like "normal" and "abnormal," "true" and "false," and "real" and "fake." Such distinctions do not lend themselves to argument. They are proffered to us as axiomatic truths, as empirical facts which no normal person would ever dream of contradicting.

In place of competing political philosophies, the neoliberal intelligentsia is substituting a simpler choice, "normality" or "abnormality." The nature of the "abnormality" varies according to what is being stigmatized. Today it's "Corbyn the anti-Semite," tomorrow it's "Sanders the racist crackpot," or "Trump the Manchurian candidate," or whatever. That the smears themselves are indiscriminate (and, in many instances, totally ridiculous) belies the effectiveness of the broader strategy, which is simply to abnormalize the target and whatever he or she represents. It makes no difference whether one is smeared as a racist, as Sanders was during the primaries, or an anti-Semite, as Corbyn has been, or a fascist, as Trump has relentlessly been, or as peddlers of Russian propaganda, as *Truthout, CounterPunch*, *Naked Capitalism*, and a number of other publications have been … the message is, they are somehow "not normal."

Why is this any different from the shameless smear jobs the press has been doing on people since the invention of the press and shameless smear jobs? Well, hold on, because I'm about to tell you.

Mostly it has to do with words, especially binary oppositions like "real" and "fake," and "normal" and "abnormal," which are, of course,

13 "The Pathologization of Dissent," CounterPunch, October 27, 2016

essentially meaningless … their value being purely tactical. Which is to say they denote nothing. They are weapons deployed by a dominant group to enforce conformity to its consensus reality. This is how they're being used at the moment.

The meaningless binary oppositions that the neoliberal intelligentsia and the corporate media are supplanting traditional opposing political philosophies with (i.e., normal/abnormal, real/fake), in addition to stigmatizing a diversity of sources of non-conforming information and ideas, are also restructuring our consensus reality as a conceptual territory in which anyone thinking, writing, or speaking outside the mainstream is deemed some kind of "deviant," or "extremist," or some other form of social pariah. Again, it doesn't matter what kind, as "deviance" in itself is the point.

Actually, the opposite of deviance is the point. Because this is how "normality" is manufactured. And how consensus reality as a whole is manufactured … and how the manufacturing process is concealed.

The media's current obsession with "fake news" conceals the fact that there is no "real news," and simultaneously produces "real news," or, rather, the simulation thereof. It does so by means of the binary opposition (i.e., if such a thing as "fake news" exists … then, ipso facto, "real news" exists). Likewise, the focus on "not normalizing Trump" conceals the fact that there is no "normality," and simultaneously manufactures "normality" … which is always only a simulation.

Similarly, the stigmatization of Trump as a modern-day Hitler, or Mussolini, or some other type of fascist dictator, conceals the fact that the United States is already virtually a one-party system, with concentrated ownership and control of the media, an omnipresent militarized police force, arbitrary enforcement of the rule of law, the maintenance of a more or less permanent state of war, and many other standard features of authoritarian systems of government. At the same time, this projection of "fascism" conjures, or manufactures, its opposite, "democracy" … or the simulation of democracy.

This neoliberal simulation of democracy, and normality, and reality, is what the corporate media, and the entire neoliberal intelligentsia, is desperately working to shore up at the moment, as they took quite a hit with this election mess. Trump was not supposed to win. He was supposed to be another Hitlerian bogeyman that the neoliberals could save us all from, but then ... well, look what happened.

The problem for the neoliberal ruling classes, and the mainstream media, and liberals generally, having gone balls out on the Hitler schtick, is that they pretty much have to keep it up now, which is going to get increasingly weird as Trump turns out to not be Hitler, but, rather, just another Republican plutocrat, albeit one with zero government experience and some certified bull goose loonies on his staff. I'm sure Trump will want to help them out, though (i.e., his neoliberal "enemies"), with the occasional racist or misogynist tweet, as he will need to maintain his "white working class" creds, at least until the "War on Islam" gets going.

In any event, we can all look forward to some serious pathologization of dissent throughout the next four (and perhaps eight) years. And I'm not referring to Trump and his boys, though I'm certain they'll be in there slinging it too. I'm referring to our friends in the corporate media, like Marty Baron and his smear machine, and the Guardians of Reality at *The New York Times*, *The Guardian*, and other "papers of record."

WNYC is already airing a daily "descent into fascism" segment. And of course the neoliberal left, *Mother Jones*, *The Nation*, et al., and *The New York Review of Books*, apparently, (they just can't get enough of this Hitler stuff) will be monitoring liberals' every thought to ensure that fascism does not get normalized ... which, God have mercy should that ever happen. Who knows what America might end up doing? Torturing people? Attacking other countries that pose no threat to it whatsoever? Indefinitely imprisoning people in camps? Assassinating anyone the president deems a "terrorist" or an "enemy combatant" with the tacit approval of the majority of Americans? Surveilling everyone's phone calls, emails, tweets, and reading and web-browsing habits?

Imagine the dystopia we would all be living in ... if things like that were considered "normal."

Why Ridiculous Propaganda Still Works

January 13, 2017

For students of official propaganda, manipulation of public opinion, psychological conditioning, and emotional coercion, it doesn't get much better than this. As Trump and his army of Goldman Sachs guys, corporate CEOs, and Christian zealots slouch toward inauguration day, we are being treated to a master class in coordinated media manipulation that is making Goebbels look like an amateur. This may not be immediately apparent, given the seemingly risible nature of most of the garbage we are being barraged with, but once one understands the actual purpose of official propaganda, everything starts to make more sense.

Chief among the common misconceptions about the way official propaganda works is the notion that its goal is to deceive the public into believing things that are not "the truth" (that Trump is a Russian agent, for example, or that Saddam had weapons of mass destruction, or that the terrorists hate us for our freedom, et cetera). However, while official propagandists are definitely pleased if anyone actually believes whatever lies they are selling, deception is not their primary aim.

The primary aim of official propaganda is to generate an "official narrative" that can be mindlessly repeated by the ruling classes and those who support and identify with them. This official narrative does not have to make sense, or to stand up to any sort of serious scrutiny. Its factualness is not the point. The point is to draw a Maginot line, a defensive ideological boundary, between "the truth" as defined by the ruling classes and any other "truth" that contradicts their narrative.

Imagine this Maginot line as a circular wall surrounded by inhospitable territory. Inside the wall is "normal" society, gainful employment, career advancement, and all the other considerable benefits of cooperating with the ruling classes. Outside the wall is poverty, anxiety, social and professional stigmatization, and various other forms of suffering. Which side of the wall do you want to be on? Every day, in countless ways, each of us are asked and have to answer this question. Conform, and there's a place for you inside. Refuse, and ... well, good luck out there.

In openly despotic societies, the stakes involved in making this choice (to conform or dissent) are often life and death. In our relatively liberal Western societies (for those of us who are not militant guerillas), the consequences of not conforming to the official narrative are usually subtler. Despite that, the pressure is still intense. Conforming to the consensus "reality" generated by these official narratives is price of admission to the inner sanctum, where the jobs, money, professional prestige, and the other rewards of capitalism are. Conforming does not require belief. It requires allegiance and rote obedience. What one actually believes is completely irrelevant, as long as one parrots the official narrative.

In short, official propaganda is not designed to deceive the public (no more than the speeches in an actor's script are intended to deceive the actor who speaks them). It is designed to be absorbed and repeated, no matter how implausible or preposterous it might be. Actually, it is often most effective when those who are forced to robotically repeat it know that it is utter nonsense, as the humiliation of having to do so cements their allegiance to the ruling classes (this phenomenon being a standard feature of the classic Stockholm Syndrome model, and authoritarian conditioning generally).

The current "Russian hacking" hysteria is a perfect example of how this works. No one aside from total morons actually believes this official narrative (the substance of which is beyond ridiculous), not even the stooges selling it to us. This, however, is not a problem, because it isn't intended to be believed. It is intended to be accepted and repeated, more or less like religious dogma. (It doesn't matter what actually happened, i.e., whether the "hack" was a hack or a leak, or who the hackers or leakers were, or who they may have been working for, or what whoever's motives may have been. What matters is that the ruling classes have issued a new official narrative and are demanding that every "normal" American stand up and swear allegiance to it.)

The ruling classes are not exactly making it easy for their followers this time. Their new official narrative (let's go ahead and call it "The Putinist Putsch to Destroy Democracy") is so completely fatuous that it's beyond embarrassing. The plot is more or less what you'd expect from a mediocre young adult novel or a Game of Thrones-type fantasy series. And if that wasn't already humiliating enough for the liberals being asked to pretend to believe it, the PR folks in charge couldn't even be bothered to assemble a new collection of liars to market their childish fairy tale for them. Not only are they insisting that liberals take the word of the "Intelligence Community" and the mainstream media that sold the world the "Saddam Has Secret WMDs" hoax, they actually dispatched James R. Clapper to sit there, in more or less the same exact spot he sat in the last time he lied to Congress, and do his dog and pony show again.

Meanwhile, the ruling classes' papers of record, which cosmopolitan liberals rely on to provide a simulation of "serious journalism," highbrow "arts and culture," and so on, have descended to the level of the *National Enquirer*. Among the highlights was *The Washington Post*'s "Russians Hacked the Vermont Power Grid" story,[1] which it turned out involved neither Russians nor hackers, nor the Vermont power grid's actual computers, and was basically just another made-up story, like the one about Putin's Fake News Army.[2] *The New York Times,* which has also been dutifully rolling out the new official narrative, has taken the leash off Charles M. Blow (aka "The Withering Gaze"[3]), who is accusing Trump of being "Russia's appointment" and

---

1 Eilperin, Juliet and Entous, Adam, "Russian operation hacked a Vermont utility, showing risk to U.S. electrical grid security, officials say," The Washington Post, December 30, 2016

2 Timberg, Craig, "Russian propaganda effort helped spread fake news during election, experts say," The Washington Post, November 24, 2016

3 Blow, Charles M., "No, Trump, We Can't Just Get Along," The New York Times, November 23, 2016 ("You are a fraud and a charlatan. Yes, you will be president, but you will not get any breaks just because one branch of your forked tongue is silver ... I have not only an ethical and professional duty to call out how obscene your very existence is at the top of American government; I have a moral obligation to do so ... so let me say this on Thanksgiving: I'm thankful to have this platform because as long as there are ink and pixels, you will be the focus of my withering gaze.")

proclaiming his election "an act of war."[4] And now, as I was writing this piece, they hit us with the "Golden Showers" story, in which Trump paid a bunch of Russian hookers to pee on the bed where Obama once slept.[5] Any day now we are going to be told that Elvis is secretly working with Putin to deploy a Zhirinovskian gravitational weapon in a UFO disguised as Jesus that Assange and Snowden will personally pilot across the Atlantic to sink America. It's like some kind of loyalty test in which the ruling classes are trying to determine just how far they can go with this crap before liberals refuse to salute any more of it.

The point of all this propaganda is to delegitimize Donald Trump, and to prophylactically reassert the neoliberal ruling classes' monopoly on power, "reality," and "truth." In case this wasn't already abundantly clear, the neoliberal ruling classes have no intention of giving up control of the global capitalist pseudo-empire they've been working to establish these last sixty years. They're going to delegitimize and stigmatize Trump (and any other symbol of nationalist backlash or resistance to transnational capitalism), bide their time for the next four years, and then install another of their loyal servants … after which life will go back to "normal," and liberals will do their best to forget this unfortunate period where they pretended to believe this insipid neo-McCarthyite nonsense.

If I wasn't worried that Trump was going to launch an all-out War on Islam, or that one of "our boys" in the tanks Obama has theatrically ordered to the Russian border was going to go bonkers and try to "git some" for Clinton, I'd be looking forward to seeing just how batshit crazy it's going to get.

---

4 Blow, Charles M., "Donald Trump and the Tainted Presidency," The New York Times, January 9, 2019

5 Shane, Scott, Rosenberg, Matthew, and Goldman, Adam, "Trump Received Unsubstantiated Report That Russia Had Damaging Information About Him," The New York Times, January 10, 2017

The Resistance and Its Double

January 30, 2017

So the neoliberal ruling classes are putting on a little revolution, to which you and I are cordially invited. The occasion is the takeover of the United States by Vladimir Putin and his Manchurian President, or the official launch of the Trumpian Reich, whichever hysterical scenario you prefer. Dress is casual. Children are welcome, as this is a strictly non-violent uprising, which will take place on the weekends, mostly, so as not to interfere with school or work. Colorful signage and puppets are encouraged, but you can leave your gas mask and welder's gloves at home, as there won't be any tear gas canisters or rubber bullets coming your way.

Oh, and it will definitely be televised.

The rebellion began on January 21, the day after Trump's inauguration, when the nation's capitol was stormed by thousands of militant liberals in pink woolly hats. Michael Moore and Madonna were there, as was John Kerry, and his dog, apparently. Expletive-laden speeches were delivered. Virtue was signaled. Selfies were taken. Requiems for Saint Obama were sung.

Notwithstanding the totally unthreatening nature of the whole affair, according to Charles "The Withering Gaze" Blow, Resident Guerrilla Fighter at *The New York Times*, this was the birth of a new "dissident" movement. "This was an uprising! This was resistance!" The Withering Gaze cried out from the barricades, or from his office high above midtown Manhattan.[1]

Much of the mainstream media concurred. "The Women's March

---

1 Blow, Charles M., "We Are Dissidents; We Are Legion," The New York Times, January 23, 2017 ("Trump set forth a portentous proposition on Friday. Saturday's Women's Marches across the country and around the world answered with a thundering roar ... a stinging rebuke to the election of a man who threatens women's rights and boasts of grabbing women's genitalia ... a rebuke of bigotry and a call for equality and inclusion. This was an uprising; this was a fighting back. This was a resistance.")

will spark the resistance!" *The Guardian* assured its Jacobinian subscribers.[2] "The Resistance Rises!" proclaimed *Time*'s new cover.[3] CNN featured "The Twitter Resistance."[4] *Rolling Stone* introduced "The Leaders of the Resistance,"[5] a coalition of grassroots activists, NGOs, and business interests, but mostly it was the Pussy Hat People that were being marketed as the movement's vanguard.

Which, all right, credit where credit is due to the organizers of the Women's March. Calling it a "Women's March" (a) imbued it with a grassroots aura, (b) obscured the larger power struggle between the global neoliberal establishment and the neo-nationalist Trump regime, and (c) rendered it impossible to criticize without coming off as a misogynist creep.

What kind of monster, after all, would want to criticize millions of women dressed as vaginas and other reproductive organs for "being proactive about women's rights," and "joining in their diversity," and so on, because they accidentally happened to organize their protests in a way that perfectly aligned with the aims of the global neoliberal establishment, which is relentlessly delegitimizing Trump for reasons that have nothing to do with women? Imagine, if they had called it a "Liberals' March," or a "Deep State March," or a "March to Restore the Democrats to Power as Soon as Possible." It wouldn't have been anywhere nearly as effective, in terms of framing the official narrative.

The "Resistance" sprang into action again in response to Trump's "Muslim Ban" this weekend. Following word that he had ordered a blanket entry ban of people from a list of seven so-called "countries of concern" (that the Obama administration had identified in its Visa Waiver Program Improvement and Terrorist Travel Prevention Act of 2015, and stripped of Visa Waiver Program privileges), Michael Moore blew his Twitter horn, summoning thousands of outraged protesters to Terminal 4 of JFK Airport to militantly assemble in

---

2 Mason, Paul, "Millions have done something together – why the Women's March will spark the resistance," The Guardian, January 23, 2017

3 Hatch, Jenavieve, "Time's Powerful New Cover Reminds The World The Resistance To Trump Has Arrived," Huffington Post, January 26, 2017

4 Fiegerman, Seth, "The Twitter resistance: Fighting Trump one tweet at a time," CNN, January 27, 2017

5 Dickinson, Tim, "Meet the Leaders of the Trump Resistance," Rolling Stone, January 13, 2017

a designated area (so as not to impede the normal flow of traffic) and completely shut down an adjacent parking lot. The protests spread to airports throughout the country and "sparked "fury and anguish around the world," according to the Sunday edition of *The Guardian* (which, as of approximately 08:30 this Sunday has gone to Emergency Live-Tweet mode to cover every fascistic twist in this evolving Fall of Democracy story).

Now, before any Trumpward-leaning readers get too excited about where I'm going with this, I should probably state for the record here that I regard the man as a dangerous idiot, made even more dangerous by the fact that his program appears to be primarily the work of Steve Bannon, who is not an idiot, and is much more dangerous. I'm imagining Bannon slouched on a couch in his lair in the White House this Sunday morning, sporting his signature impish grin as he scans the reaction of the mainstream media to his latest perfectly calculated gambit. The man knows exactly what he's doing. With a stroke of Trump's pen he has simultaneously reassured his neo-nationalist base that Trump's promises were not just empty threats and provoked the media and urban liberals into an understandable but mindless frenzy of unfocused anti-Trump "resistance." This is a textbook insurrectionist tactic that Bannon has been employing with alarming success.

The reason he has been so successful is that the Trump regime and the neoliberal establishment are playing to two entirely different audiences. The Trumpians are playing to "flyover country," not just nationally, also internationally. For reasons I'll get into in more detail shortly, many of these non-urban working class folks are not real thrilled with globalism and are responding to Trump's neo-nationalist message. The neoliberal elites are playing to their base, most of whom are no less misguided than the folks they deride in "flyover country." This is mostly due to the identity politics that have been part and parcel of neoliberal ideology for going on the last fifty years, and is why the so-called "resistance" to Trump is centered around issues like racism and misogyny, rather than any kind of cogent reading of the global political dynamics at play here.

This is the problem with identity politics when divorced from a broader political discussion and over-simplified for mass consumption. By occupying the conceptual territory where any deeper or more threatening analysis of political dynamics might take place, it prevents the formation of such analysis. It answers the question "Who is fighting who?" in advance of the question being asked, in order to prevent it being asked.

So, who *is* fighting who in this case ... if it's not as simple as the forces of Love fighting the forces of Racism and Hate?

Well, here's one way of looking at it …

What we're experiencing throughout the West at the moment is a neo-nationalist insurrection against globalism. An "insurrection" because global capitalism is a global-hegemonic system. It has no viable external enemies. People, unhappy with how capitalism has been restructuring their lives since the end of the Cold War, and aware that power has been gradually shifting from sovereign nations to supranational entities, multinational corporations, international institutions, and so on, are reaching for the only alternative on offer ... neo-nationalism, in one form or another.

This is what the Trumpians and the Brexit gang are promising, a halt of the spread of global capitalism and the restoration of national sovereignty.

The neoliberal ruling classes, naturally, would like to prevent this from happening. Which, make no mistake, they are going to do (although they may let Trump, Bannon, et al. go ahead and have their War on Islam to finish destabilizing the Middle East first). What is being marketed to us as the "resistance to Trump," technically, is a counter-insurgency operation … the global neoliberal establishment quashing the neo-nationalist uprising. But that kind of thing doesn't sell very well. What sells much better is Hitler hysteria, neo-McCarthyite propaganda, and emotionally loaded trigger words that short-circuit any kind of critical thinking, words like "love," "hate," "racism," "fascism," "normal," and of course "resistance."

The irony is, the actual resistance (if the word "resistance" still has any meaning) is the one being waged by the neo-nationalists, who are, in fact, resisting something, namely neoliberalism, which is clearly the dominant force in this equation. This doesn't make them any more righteous, unless you're in favor of racism, sexism, theocracy, and other such despotic values.

"Resistance" is not a virtue in itself. Its virtue depends on who is doing the resisting, and what they're resisting, and on various other sociopolitical and historical factors that won't fit into a tweet or a sound bite.

In any event, the quandary folks on the Left are currently facing is twofold: (1) how to oppose the Trumpians, and other neo-nationalist insurgencies, without serving the interests of neoliberalism; and (2) how to oppose neoliberalism without serving the interests of the neo-nationalists. Which is more or less a classic Zen koan designed to make one's head explode.

Both the neoliberals and the neo-nationalists know this, and will be using this quandary to pressure us into joining their respective camps. Until this insurrection is neutralized, and the Trumpians are either removed from office or tamed (which at this point seems rather unlikely), the Neoliberal Liberation Army will be barraging us on a daily basis with news of the imminent end of everything and histrionic entreaties to "resist."

Meanwhile, Steve Bannon (who will continue to run things while Trump obsesses over the size of his whatever) will be relentlessly pushing his agenda forward. The scary thing is, he is obviously smart enough to know that his insurrection is doomed if the fight remains merely on the economic level (i.e, trade deals, bringing back jobs, et cetera). He understands the global economy, as do the rest of Trump's Goldman Sachs team. Which means it probably won't be all that long until the War on Islam gets officially launched, as there's nothing like a war to unite a country … and manufacturing military ordnance at home won't screw with the price of people's smartphones.

Hopefully, by the time that war begins, The Withering Gaze and the Pussy Hat People (most of whom had zero qualms about Obama bombing seven Muslim countries to serve the interests of the neoliberal establishment that has been aggressively restructuring the Middle East since the end of the Cold War with total impunity) will have morphed into an actual revolutionary army, one that doesn't get decommissioned whenever a Democrat moves into the White House, but I kind of have my doubts about that.

Goose-stepping Our Way Toward Pink Revolution

February 21, 2017

So, the global capitalist ruling classes' neutralization of the Trumpian uprising seems to be off to a pretty good start. It's barely been a month since his inauguration, and the corporate media, liberal celebrities, and their millions of faithful fans and followers are already shrieking for his summary impeachment, or his removal by ... well, whatever means necessary, including some sort of "deep-state" coup. Words like "treason" are being bandied about,[1] treason being grounds for impeachment (not to mention being punishable by death), which appears to be where we're headed at this point.

In any event, the nation is now officially in a state of "crisis." The editors of *The New York Times* are demanding congressional investigations to root out the Russian infiltrators who have assumed control of the executive branch. According to prize-winning economist Paul Krugman, "a foreign dictator intervened on behalf of a US presidential candidate," so "we are being governed by people who take their cues from Moscow," or some such nonsense.[2] *The Washington Post*, CNN, MSNBC, *The Guardian*, *The New Yorker*, *Politico*, *Mother Jones*, et al. (in other words virtually every organ of the Western neoliberal media) are robotically repeating this propaganda like the Project Mayhem cultists in Fight Club.[3]

---

1 Devega, Chauncey, "None dare call it treason: As the Flynn scandal widens, let's consider the evidence that Trump is a traitor," Slate, February 16, 2017

2 Krugman, Paul, "The Silence of the Hacks," The New York Times, February 17, 2017

3 Miller, Greg, Entous, Adam and Nakashima, Ellen, "National security advisor Flynn discussed sanctions with Russian ambassador despite denials, officials say," The Washington Post, February 9, 2017; Brown, Pamela, Sciutto, Jim, and Perez, Evan, "Trump aides were in constant touch with senior Russian officials during campaign," CNN, February 16, 2017; Benen, Steve, "New questions surround Team Trump's pre-election talks with Russia," MSNBC, February 15, 2017; Jacobs, Ben

The fact that there is not one shred of actual evidence to support these claims makes absolutely no difference whatsoever. As I pointed out in these pages previously,[4] official propaganda is not designed to be credible; it is designed to bludgeon people into submission through sheer relentless repetition and fear of social ostracization ... which, once again, is working perfectly. Like the "Iraq has WMDs" narrative before it, the "Putin Hacked the Election" narrative has now become official "reality," an unchallengeable axiomatic "fact" which can be cited as background to pretend to bolster additional ridiculous propaganda.

This "Russia Hacked the Election" narrative, let's remember, was generated by a series of stories that it turned out were either completely fabricated or based on "anonymous intelligence sources" that could provide no evidence, "for reasons of security."

Who could forget *The Washington Post*'s "Russian Propagandists Blacklist" story[5] (which was based on the claims of some anonymous' blog), or their "Russians Hacked the Vermont Power Grid" story[6] (which, it turned out later, was totally made up), or CNN's "Golden Showers Dossier" story[7] (which was the work of some ex-MI6 spook-for-hire the Never Trump folks had on their payroll), or *Slate*'s "Trump's Russian Server" story[8] (a half-assed smear piece by Franklin Foer, who is now pretending to have been vindicated by the hysteria over the Flynn resignation), or (and this is my personal favorite) *The Washington Post*'s "Clinton Poisoned by Putin" story?[9]

---

and Ackerman, Spencer, "Trump decries 'criminal' leaks exposing Michael Flynn's Russia cover-up," The Guardian, February 15, 2017; Cassidy, John, "It's Time for a Proper Investigation of Trump's Russia Ties," The New Yorker, February 14, 2017; Nussbaum, Matthew, "Trump raises specter of 'nuclear holocaust' while talking Russia," Politico, February 16, 2017; Corn, David, "Why Trump Can't Come Clean on Russia," Mother Jones, February 14, 2017

4 "Why Ridiculous Propaganda Still Works," CounterPunch, January 13, 2017

5 Timberg, Craig, "Russian propaganda effort helped spread fake news during election, experts say," The Washington Post, November 24, 2016

6 Eilperin, Juliet and Entous, Adam, "Russian operation hacked a Vermont utility, showing risk to U.S. electrical grid security, officials say," The Washington Post, December 30, 2016

7 Shane, Scott, Rosenberg, Matthew, and Goldman, Adam, "Trump Received Unsubstantiated Report That Russia Had Damaging Information About Him," The New York Times, January 10, 2017

8 Foer, Franklin, "Was a Trump Server Communicating With Russia?" Slate, October 31, 2016

9 Boren, Cindy, "The Man Who Discovered CTE Thinks Hillary Clinton Might Have Been Poisoned," The Washington Post, September 12, 2016

Who could possibly forget these examples of courageous journalists speaking truth to power?

Well, OK, a lot of people, apparently, because there's been a new twist in the official narrative. It seems the capitalist ruling classes now need us to defend the corporate media from the tyrannical criticism of Donald Trump, or else ... well, you know, end of democracy.

Which millions of people are actually doing. Seriously, absurd as it obviously is, millions of Americans are now rushing to defend the most fearsome propaganda machine in the history of fearsome propaganda machines from one inarticulate, populist boogeyman who can't maintain his train of thought for more than fifteen or twenty seconds.

All joking aside, the prevailing mindset of the ruling classes, and those aspiring thereto, is more frightening than at any time I can remember. "The Resistance" is exhibiting precisely the type of mindlessly fascistic, herd-like behavior it purports to be trying to save us from. The mood in Twitter Resistance quarters has turned quite openly authoritarian. William Kristol captured it succinctly:

> "Obviously strongly prefer normal democratic and constitutional politics. But if it comes to it, [I] prefer the deep state to the Trump state."

Rob "Meathead" Reiner put it this way:

> "The incompetent lying narcissistic fool is going down. Intelligence community will not let [Trump] destroy democracy."

Subcommandante Micheal Moore went to the caps lock to drive the point home:

> "It doesn't take a rocket scientist to figure out what was going on: TRUMP COLLUDING WITH THE RUSSIANS TO THROW THE ELECTION TO HIM ..."

And demanded that Trump be immediately detained and renditioned to a secure facility:

> "... let's be VERY clear: Flynn DID NOT make that Russian call on his own. He was INSTRUCTED to do so. He was TOLD to reassure them. Arrest Trump."

These a just a few of the more sickening examples. The point is, millions of American citizens (as well as citizens of other countries) are prepared to support a deep-state coup to remove the elected president from office.

It doesn't get much more fascistic than that.

Now, I want to be clear about this "deep state" business, as the mainstream media is already labeling anyone who uses the term a hopelessly paranoid conspiracy theorist.

The deep state, of course, is not a conspiracy. It is simply the interdependent network of structures where actual power resides (i.e., the military-industrial complex, multinational corporations, Wall Street, the corporate media, and so on). Its purpose is to maintain the stability of the system regardless of which party controls the government. These are the folks, when a president takes office, who show up and brief him on what is and isn't "possible" given economic and political "realities."

Despite what Alex Jones might tell you, it is not George Soros and a roomful of Jews. It is a collection of military and intelligence agency officers, CEOs, corporate lobbyists, lawyers, bankers, politicians, power brokers, aides, advisers, and assorted other permanent members of the government and the corporate and financial classes. Just as presidents come and go, so do the individuals comprising the deep state, albeit on a longer rotation schedule. And, thus, it is not a monolithic entity. Like any other decentralized network, it contains contradictions and conflicts of interest. However, what remains a constant is the deep state's commitment to preserving the system ... which, in our case, that system is global capitalism.

I'm going to repeat and italicize that to hopefully avoid any misunderstanding. The system the deep state primarily serves is not the United States of America, i.e., the country most Americans believe they live in; *the system it serves is globalized capitalism.* The United States, the nation state itself, while obviously a crucial element of the system, is not the deep state's primary concern. If it were, Americans would all have healthcare, affordable education, and a right to basic housing, like more or less every other developed nation.

And this is the essence of the present conflict. The Trump regime (whether they're sincere or not) have capitalized on people's discontent with globalized neoliberal capitalism, which is doing away with outmoded concepts like the nation state and national sovereignty and restructuring the world into one big marketplace where "Chinese" investors own "American" companies that manufacture goods for "European" markets by paying "Thai" workers three dollars a day to enrich "American" hedge fund crooks whose "British" bankers stash their loot in numbered accounts in the Cayman Islands, while "American" workers pay their taxes so that the "United States" can give billions of dollars to "Israelis" and assorted terrorist outfits that are destabilizing the Middle East to open up markets for the capitalist ruling classes, who have no allegiance to any country, and who couldn't possibly care any less about the common people who have to live there.

Trump supporters, rubes that they are, don't quite follow the logic of all that, or see how it benefits them or their families.

But whatever ... they're all just fascists, right? And we're in a state of crisis, aren't we? This is not the time to sit around and analyze political and historical dynamics. No, this is a time for all loyal Americans to set aside their critical thinking and support democracy, the corporate media, and the NSA, and CIA, and the rest of the deep state (which doesn't exist) as they take whatever measures are necessary to defend us from Putin's diabolical plot to Nazify the United States and reenact the Holocaust for no discernible reason.

The way things are going, it's just a matter of time until they either impeach his puppet, Trump, or ... you know, remove him by other means. I imagine, once we get to that point, Official State Satirist Stephen Colbert will cover the proceedings live on the "Late Show," whipping his studio audience up into a frenzy of mindless patriotic merriment, as he did in the aftermath of the Flynn fiasco (accusing the ruling classes' enemies of treason being the essence of political satire, of course).[10] After he's convicted and dying in jail,[11] triumphant Americans will pour onto the lawn of Lafayette Square again, waving huge flags and hooting vuvuzelas, like they did when Obama killed Osama bin Laden.

I hope you'll forgive me if I don't attend. Flying home might be a little complicated, as according to *The Washington Post*, I'm some kind of Russian propagandist now. And, also, I have this problem with authority, which I don't imagine will go over very well with whatever provisional government is installed to oversee the Restoration of Normality, and Love, of course, throughout the nation.

10 Guardian staff, "Late-night TV hosts skewer Michael Flynn: 'It's funny 'cause it's treason'," The Guardian, February 15, 2017

11 Schindler, John, "Now we go nuclear. IC war going to new levels. Just got an EM fm senior IC friend, it began: "He will die in jail." Twitter, February 15, 2017

The United States of Cognitive Dissonance

March 23, 2017

It's always somewhat sad and confusing when a massive propaganda campaign like the one we've been subjected to for about the last year comes to a sudden and ignominious end. You wake up one morning, and the billionaire asshat that more or less every "respected" organ of the corporate media has been telling you was Hitler, or a Russian agent, and possibly both, as it turns out, is ... well, just a billionaire asshat. An extremely repulsive billionaire asshat, but nonetheless just a billionaire asshat. This is very disorienting, because here you were, prepped for the End of Everything, or at least for the death camps, the Riefenstahlian rallies, and the Russian invasion of Martha's Vineyard, and then all that stuff gets abruptly canceled like Season 4 of David Milch's *Deadwood*.

We haven't quite reached that stage of things yet, but it feels like we are inching up to it (as Glenn Greenwald pointed out in his recent piece[1]). I know this sounds a little nuts, given the amount of Russia hysteria the media is pumping out this week as the KremlinGate hearings get underway, but this latest round of official propaganda distinctly reeks of desperation.

The simple fact of the matter is, despite whatever got "hacked" by whom, Donald Trump, asshat that he is, is not a Russian sleeper agent or otherwise collaborating with Vladimir Putin, and anyone with half a brain knows this. Thus, it is going to be impossible to prove the blatantly ridiculous accusations the ruling classes and their media stooges have been making in order to delegitimize him. This is going to present a problem, because the way it works, when you accuse the president of treason (which is a capital offense) is that you kind of have to prove it at some point. The ruling classes cannot do

---

1 Greenwald, Glenn, "Key Democratic Officials Now Warning Base Not to Expect Evidence of Trump/Russia Collusion," The Intercept, March 16, 2017

this, and thus they need to adjust expectations, which is what they appear to be doing at the moment.

As Greenwald noted in his *Intercept* piece, deep-state disinformation specialists like Michael Morrell and James R. Clapper are making the rounds of the talk shows and forums, preparing us for the official narrative changeover. You remember Michael Morrell … the ex-CIA chief who in August of last year wrote that op-ed in *The New York Times* declaring that "Putin had recruited Trump as an unwitting agent of the Russian Federation."[2]

And it is not only spooks like Morrell and Clapper. Suddenly, the oracles we've to come rely on for the latest evidence that Putin-Nazis have taken over the executive branch are adopting a distinctly less hysterical tone. Although they haven't kicked the Russia paranoia cold turkey (as that might cause mass seizures or something), they have obviously begun to wean their followers off the groundless neo-McCarthyite nonsense they've been peddling straight-faced for over a year.

Paul "It's the 1930s Again" Krugman has turned his attention back to budgets and taxes, and has toned down both the "Return of Fascism"[3] and the "We Are Being Governed by Moscow"[4] schtick. *The Washington Post*, the paper that brought us not only the "Putin Hacks Vermont" story,[5] but the "Anyone who Criticizes Hillary Clinton is a Russian Propagandist" story,[6] is also going lighter on the blatant smear jobs, and focusing on stuff like how much former Hitler's vacations are costing the taxpayer. Even a shameless tabloid like *The Guardian* is doing its part to dampen expections.[7] With notable exceptions (like Rachel Maddow, Louise Mensch,[8] and other

---

2 Morell, Michael, "I Ran the C.I.A. Now I'm Endorsing Hillary Clinton," The New York Times, August 5, 2016

3 Krugman, Paul, "How Republics End," The New York Times, December 19, 2016

4 Krugman, Paul, "The Silence of the Hacks," The New York Times, February 17, 2017

5 Eilperin, Juliet and Entous, Adam, "Russian operation hacked a Vermont utility, showing risk to U.S. electrical grid security, officials say," The Washington Post, December 30, 2016

6 Timberg, Craig, "Russian propaganda effort helped spread fake news during election, experts say," The Washington Post, November 24, 2016

7 Harding, Luke, "What we know – and what's true – about the Trump-Russia dossier," The Guardian, January 11, 2017

8 Mensch, Louise, "What to Ask About Russian Hacking, The New York Times, March 17, 2017 (Seriously, the editors of The New York Times actually gave Mensch a prominent op-ed spot)

bull goose loonies), the Arbiters of Reality seem to be settling in for a protracted battle, as opposed to the impeachment proceedings or deep-state coup they've been openly pining for. The overriding message is … "Don't expect any proof of Trump's collusion with Russia, but that doesn't mean he didn't do it, and it doesn't really matter if we can't prove it, because even if we can't officially impeach him, he's still a fascist, Putin-loving traitor, and since we're stuck with him for the next four years, we're going to move on to other things."

All of which is understandably jarring for the neoliberals, neoconservatives, and just garden variety authoritarians who've been dutifully swallowing the preposterous swill the corporate media has been pouring down their throats (and who have been looking forward to Trump's removal from office). And more so, given that, in the course of a year, they have (a) had to pretend to believe that Donald Trump is a modern-day Hitler who is going to exterminate millions of people and transform America into a new Fourth Reich, and then (b) once that tactic didn't work, immediately forget the Hitler hooey, and pretend to believe that Donald Trump is a secret agent working for Putin, who they (c) suddenly had to believe is an evil James Bond-villian-type menace intent on annihilating Western democracy … all of which has been hard to swallow, given that, just before all this started, they (d) were just getting used to believing that the official enemy was not Putin, or fascists, but rather, those scary self-radicalized terrorists.

Can you remember back to when they were the enemy (i.e., the "suddenly self-radicalized terrorists")? It was actually less than a year ago. The media was calling it "The Summer of Fear."[9] Back then, Trump was just becoming Hitler — they had started with the Hitler stuff back in May — but Putin wasn't controlling him yet, as no one thought he had a chance of defeating Clinton in the general election, so the terrorists were still the reigning bogeymen,and George W. Bush was still a war criminal and not smooching it up with Ellen DeGeneres.

If all that sounds impossible to follow, and totally insane, that's because it is … and is how Americans, and not just Americans, but

9 Connolly, Kate and Willsher, Kim, "Summer of fear: the anxious mood in Germany and France, The Guardian, July 29, 2016

mostly Americans, are being conditioned to think ... or, rather, to react to a disjunctive series of totally nonsensical emotional stimuli, like the subject of some sick psychological experiment.

Let's take a moment and visualize this ...

Imagine the subject strapped in a chair like Alex was in *Clockwork Orange*, barraged with images of frightening terrorists until his mind accepts them as "the enemy," at which point "the enemy" is immediately switched, and now it's Hitler that is coming to get him, which, after a time, he comes to accept (and forgets the former terrorist "enemy"), at which point "the enemy" is switched again, and now it's Putin and the Russians who are after him.

And so on, until his mind just snaps and surrenders to whatever official "reality" is being fed into it any given day. At which point you have rendered the subject a totally compliant, scramble-headed, functionally psychotic member of society, whose attention span is about twenty seconds, and whose brain you can fill full of fancy pharmaceuticals to keep it from completely melting down in response to the stress of the cognitive dissonance that it has to deal with on a daily basis.

Orwell captured this cognitive dissonance in the chapter of *1984* where the Party executes the sudden switch from war with Eurasia to war with Eastasia. Unfortunately, we are way past Orwell. The neoliberal ruling classes are not simply switching official enemies; *they're switching the nature of the same official enemy*. One day, Trump is a modern-day Hitler, the next day he's a Russian agent, the day after that he's something else. To achieve the fully psychotic effect, it's the same so-called "respectable journalists" who are one day assuring us he's literally Hitler, and the next day, no, he isn't Hitler, but he's absolutely a Russian agent, and the next, OK, maybe not, but at least he's a liar, or a tax cheat, or something.

In case you were wondering, this is also how, if you're running some sort of Manson-like cult, you twist the minds of your fledgling cult members until they don't know what to believe anymore. It's pretty much Mind Control 101. You bombard their minds with conflicting realities and contradictory information until they're rendered incapable of thinking critically. Then you fill their heads with whatever brand of psycho nonsense your cult is peddling.

I'm not kidding. Check this out. There's all kind of literature that explains how this works. Or, if you don't have time to do that, just call someone at *The New York Times*, *The Guardian*, or *The Washington Post*, or CNN, or MSNBC. I'm sure they'll be more than happy to explain the whole "anti-Semitic, staunchly Zionist, Wall Street-friendly, anti-Wall Street, moronically cunning, inarticulately mesmerizing, blackmailed by and profiting from Russia, Putin-Nazi puppet" thing to you. But you may want to drop some acid first in order to get the full effect.

The President Formerly Known as Hitler

April 21, 2017

So, the President formerly known as Hitler has apparently pulled his head out of his ass and gotten with the global capitalist program. The ruling classes couldn't be more relieved, as it was beginning to look like they were going to have to carry on with their totally ridiculous "Manchurian President" propaganda indefinitely, or deal with Trump in some harsher way, which, given the paranoid mood in the country and the heavily-armed nature of a lot of his supporters, was going to get a little tricky.

Forunately, however, H.R. McMaster, James Mattis, and the rest of the permanent members of the global capitalist war machine (better known as the United States military), as well as his bleeding heart daughter, Ivanka, were able to talk some sense into Trump, and convince him to employ about sixty cruise missiles to pointlessly obliterate a Syrian airstrip, and then drop a $314 million Massive Ordnance Air Blast bomb on a few dozen "terrorists" in some caves in Afghanistan.

The fact that these air strikes had virtually zero military value was beside the point. The global capitalist ruling classes needed Trump to demonstrate that he is ready and willing to continue the wholesale restructuring of the Middle East that they've been carrying out since the end of the Cold War, and to bomb whatever they tell him to bomb, and, basically, to do what the fuck he's told when it comes to geopolitical matters.

Trump, who was probably tired of losing, and being referred to as Steve Bannon's puppet, and being accused of treason, and so on, and who never really gave two shits about the suckers he conned into voting for him anyway, had one of those Road to Damascus experiences, and gave the Pentagon boys carte blanche.

The display of overwhelming force that followed, at 08:40 EST,

April 6, 2017, signaled the start of the Trumpian reign. CNN talking head Fareed Zakaria put it this way the following evening:

> "I think Donald Trump became president of the United States last night … for the first time really as president, he talked about international norms, international rules, about America's role in enforcing justice in the world."[1]

This was approximately 24 hours after CNN and the other totally objective members of the mainstream media had had a chance to calm down a little, and to clean up after the orgy of obsequious cheerleading they had indulged in the previous evening. For most of the spastic talking heads who are paid to repeat whatever some producer whispers into their earpieces around the clock while making weird faces, the footage of those turgid Tomahawk missiles rising angrily out of their silos on their way to violently penetrate the enemy and explode in shuddering spasms of global corporatist power was literally orgasmic.

Pent-up editorialists instantly pumped out geysers of overwhelming approval.[2] MSNBC's Brian Williams lost it and started raving on camera about "the beauty of our fearsome armaments,"[3] and quoting Leonard Cohen, and so on. *The Washington Post* immediately brought in Robert Kagan to froth at the mouth about "rebalancing Syria in America's favor."[4]

And it wasn't just the US press and the corporate-owned US political establishment. The rest of the global capitalist empire (Germany, France, the United Kingdom, the European Council, Spain, Italy, Israel, Turkey, Saudi Arabia, et al.) were quick to cheer Trump's transformation into a grown-up, moderate, more or less rational, or at least obedient, globalist puppet.

---

1 Hensch, Mark, "CNN host: 'Donald Trump became president' last night," The Hill, April 7, 2017

2 Johnson, Adam, "Out of 47 Major Editorials on Trump's Syria Strikes, Only One Opposed," Fairness & Accuracy in Reporting, April 11, 2017

3 Smith, Allen, "MSNBC anchor Brian Williams sets off online firestorm with long soliloquy about 'beautiful' footage of missile launch in Syria," Business Insider, April 7, 2017

4 Kagan, Robert, "It'll take more than a missile strike to clean up Obama's mess in Syria," The Washington Post, April 7, 2017

Now, I owe Trump an apology at this point, because his sudden conversion to the Globalist faith proves that he is not the total ass hat I've accused him of being for twenty-five years, or at least that he is not suicidal. Prior to his soul-searching talk with Ivanka, and his chat with the generals, and to viewing the photos of those "beautiful babies" gassed by Assad in a last-ditch attempt to force the U.S. to invade his country and hang him to death, he (i.e., Trump, not Bashar al-Assad) was on the verge of a massive heart attack, or a stroke, or other medical event, or just accidentally getting shot in the head by some mentally unstable, three-named gunman. Or maybe *The New York Times*' guest loony, the increasingly Strangelovian Louise Mensch, was going to uncover a grainy VHS tape of Trump and Putin in their BDSM-wear signing a pact to destroy America in the urine of a Muscovite prostitute … or whatever.

The point is, Trump was playing with fire, having misunderstood his job description. For a while there, it seemed he actually believed that he was going to defy the will of all those "global elites" he'd been railing against (and, no, I'm not referring to "the Jews," I'm referring to the global capitalist establishment and the armies they employ to keep them in power).

This, of course, was never going to happen. The global capitalist ruling classes can put up with a lot from a U.S. president (who is the most powerful man in the world, after all), but there *are* a few lines one does not cross, and some fundamental responsibilities they need to know are going to get handled. Playing neo-nationalist grab-ass (or selling the world some Hope and Change crap) is all fine and good when you are out on the hustings, but as Obama noted on his way out of town, "reality has a way of asserting itself."[5] Or, as corporatist puppet Chuck Schumer put it, "you take on the intelligence community — they have six ways from Sunday of getting back at you."[6]

I don't mean to be overly dramatic, but we're talking about the U.S. military, CIA, NSA, and the rest of the military industrial complex.

---

5 "Barack Obama: Donald Trump will soon face sobering 'reality check' on his most controversial policies," The Independent, November 15, 2016

6 Chaitin, Daniel, "Schumer warns Trump: Intel officials 'have six ways from Sunday at getting back at you'," Washington Examiner, January 3, 2017

These are people who have no problem murdering entire families by day and going home and playing with their kids at night. Did anyone really think they were going to allow some word-salad-babbling billionaire to screw around with their long-term objectives because he happened to win a presidential election?

In any event, the danger has passed. Trump, having assumed the mantle of Commander in Chief of Global Capitalism's Worldwide Arbitrary Killing Machine (and with Cohn and the usual Goldman Sachs guys making sure he doesn't go nuts and start screwing around with their continuing efforts to transform the planet into one big, happy, neo-feudalist theme park prison), can relax and focus on improving his golf swing. Whatever mess he makes of the country (i.e., the United States of America, the nominally sovereign nation state that most Americans believe they live in) will be tolerated by the global capitalist establishment, as they couldn't care less about actual Americans, or Brits, or Greeks, or Syrians, or whoever. We're all just a bunch of cannon fodder, and servants, and deplorables, and losers, to them.

If it's any consolation, at least we'll be able to get back to "normality," finally. Yes, it will likely take a few weeks for liberals to fully recover from the shock of the cancellation of Holocaust Redux and the Imminent Invasion of the Putin-Nazis, but my prediction is, by sometime this summer, we'll have returned to more or less business as usual. That is, of course, unless Putin the Evil hacks the upcoming French elections … in which case, you know, End of Democracy, and Holocaust II, et cetera, again. Stay tuned to the corporate media for moment-by-moment updates on that.

Invasion of the Putin-Nazis

May 17, 2017

So, here we are, a little over one hundred days into "The Age of Darkness"[1] and the "racially Orwellian" Trumpian Reich,[2] and, all right, while it's certainly no party, it appears that all those rumors we heard of the Death of Neoliberalism[3] were greatly exaggerated. Not only has the entire edifice of Western democracy not been toppled, but the global capitalist ruling classes seem to be going about their business in more or less the usual manner.

The Goldman Sachs vampires are back in the White House (as they have been for over one hundred years). The post-Cold War destabilization and restructuring of the Middle East is moving forward right on schedule. The Russians, Iranians, North Koreans, and other non-globalist-ball-playing parties remain surrounded by the most ruthlessly murderous military machine in the annals of history. Greece is being debt-enslaved and looted, and so on.

Life is back to normal.

Or ... OK, not completely normal. Because, despite the fact that editorialists at "respectable" papers like *The New York Times* (and I'm explicitly referring to Charles M. Blow and Nobel Prize-winning economist Paul Krugman) have recently dropped the completely ridiculous "Trump is a Putinist agent" propaganda they'd been relentlessly spewing since he won the election, a significant number of deluded persons, having swallowed their official vomitus (i.e., the vomitus of Blow and Krugman, and other neoliberal establishment hacks) like the hungry Adélie penguin chicks in those nature shows

1 Freedland, Jonathan, "If Donald Trump wins, it'll be a new age of darkness," The Guardian, November 4, 2016

2 Blow, Charles M., "Trump: Making America White Again," The New York Times, November 21, 2016

3 Chakrabortty, Aditya, "You're witnessing the death of neoliberalism -- from within," The Guardian, May 31, 2016

narrated by David Attenborough, are convinced (i.e., these deluded persons are) that the Russians are waging a global campaign not only to maliciously hack, or interfere with, or marginally influence, free and fair elections throughout the Western world, but to control the minds of Westerners themselves, in some Orwellian, or possibly Wachowskian fashion. Worse yet, these deluded persons are certain, the Russians are now secretly running the White House, and are just using Trump and the Goldman Sachs gang, and capitalist centurions like General McMaster, as a front for their subversive activities … like denying Americans universal healthcare and privatizing the hell out of everything.

If you think I'm being hyperbolic, check out #MarchforTruth on Twitter, or its anonymous Crowdpac fundraising page,[4] which at first glance I took for an elaborate prank, but which seems to be in deadly earnest about "restoring faith in American government," uncovering Trump's "collusion" with Russia, and reversing his "subversion of the will of the people." The plan is, on June 3, 2017, thousands of otherwise rational Americans are going to pour into the streets "demanding answers" from ... well, I'm not sure whom, some independent prosecutor perhaps, or congressional committee, or intelligence agency, or whomever is responsible for ferreting out the Putin-Nazi infiltrators that respected pundits like Blow and Krugman (and stark raving loonies like Louise Mensch) have convinced them are now controlling the government.

Weirdly, these same respected journalists, the ones who have been assuring the world that The President of the United States is a covert agent working for Russia, have failed to even mention this "March for Truth," and are acting like they had nothing to do with whipping these folks up into a frenzy of apoplectic paranoia.

Incidentally, one of my colleagues contacted Mr. Blow directly and inquired as to whether he'd be vociferously supporting (or possibly leading) the March for Truth, and was chastised by Blow and his Twitter followers. I found this reaction extremely troubling, and asked my colleague to contact Mensch and suggest she check with her handlers at *The Times* to make sure the Russians haven't gotten

4 https://www.crowdpac.com/campaigns/225084/march-for-truth-june-3rd-2017 (assuming it's still up on the Internet)

to him. However, just as he was sitting down to do that, the "Comey-firing" brouhaha broke, which seems to have brought Blow back to the fold, albeit in a less hysterical manner than his Rooskie-hunting readers have grown accustomed to. We can only hope that both he and Krugman return to form in the weeks to come as Russiagate builds to its dramatic climax.

Oh, yeah, and if Russiagate isn't paranoid enough, apparently, the corporate media is now prepared to deploy the "Putin-Nazi Election Hackers" propaganda in any and every election going forward (as they did in the recent French election,[5] and as they tried to do in the Dutch elections,[6] and presumably will in the German elections, and as *The Guardian* appears to be retroactively doing in regard to the Brexit referendum).[7] Any day now, we should be hearing about the "Putin-Nazi-Corbyn Axis," and the "Putin-Nazi-Podemos Pact," and video footage of Martin Schultz and a bevy of former-East German hookers engaging in Odinist sex magick rituals in an FSB-owned bordello in Moscow. Soon, it won't just be elections … we'll be hearing reports of Russian shipments of rocks, bottles, and pointy sticks to the "Putin-Nazi Palestinian Terrorists," and … well, who knows how far they're willing to take this?

All joking aside, as I've written about previously, what we're dealing with here is more than just a lame attempt by the Democratic Party to blame its humiliating loss on Putin (although of course it certainly is that in part). The global neoliberal establishment is rolling out a new official narrative. It's actually just a slight variation on the one it's been selling us since 2001. I could come up with a sixteen-syllable, academic-sounding name for this narrative, but I'm trying to keep things simple these days … so let's call it The Normals versus The Extremists (the Normals being the neoliberals and the Extremists being everyone else).

The goal of this narrative is to stigmatize and otherwise marginalize any and all opposition to global neoliberalism, regardless of the

---

5 *Almasy, Steve, "Emmanuel Macron's French presidential campaign hacked," CNN, May 6, 2017*

6 *Chan, Sewell, "Fearful of Hacking, Dutch Will Count Ballots by Hand," The New York Times, February 1, 2017*

7 *Cadwalladr, Carole, "The great British Brexit robbery: how our democracy was hijacked," The Guardian, May 7, 2017*

nature of that opposition (i.e., whether it comes from the left, right, or from religious, environmentalist, or any other quarters).

Now, as any professional storyteller will tell you, one of the most important aspects of the narrative you're trying to suck people into is to make your protagonist a likeable underdog, and then pit him or her against a much more powerful and ideally incorrigibly evil enemy. During the Cold War, this was easy to do, as the story was Democracy versus the Commies, traditional Good versus Evil-type stuff.

However, once the U.S.S.R. collapsed, the concept needed major rewrites. A new evil adversary had to be found. This (i.e., the 1990s) was a rather awkward and frustrating period. The global capitalist ruling classes, giddy with joy after having become the first ever global ideological hegemon in the history of aspiring global hegemons, got all avant-garde for a while, and thought they could do without an "enemy." This approach, as you'll recall, did not sell well. No one quite got why we were bombing Yugoslavia, and Bush and Baker had to break out the Hitler schtick to gin up support for rescuing the Kuwaitis from their old friend Saddam.

Fortunately, in September 2001, the show runners got the break they were looking for, and the official narrative was instantly switched to Democracy versus The Islamic Terrorists. This re-brand got extremely good ratings, and would have been extended indefinitely if not for what began to unfold in the latter half of 2016. (One could go back and locate the week when the mainstream media officially switched from the "Summer of Terror" narrative they were flogging to the new "Invasion of the Putin-Nazis" narrative ... my guess is, it was early to mid-September.)

It started with the Brexit referendum, continued with the rise of Trump, and ... well, I don't have to recount it all, do I? You remember last year as clearly as I do, how, suddenly, out of seemingly nowhere, the Putin-Nazi menace materialized, and took the place of the "self-radicalized terrorist" as the primary target for people's hatred and fear. OK, sure, at first, there were no Putin-Nazis. It was just that the Brexit folks were fascists, and Trump was Hitler, and Bernie Sanders was some sort of racist hacky sack Communist. But then the Putinists poisoned Clinton, and unleashed their legions of

Russian propagandists on the gullible, Oxycodone-addicted denizens of "flyover country," and, as they say, the rest is history.

In any event, here we are, stuck inside this simulation of "reality" where Putin-Nazi hackers are coming out of the woodwork, a partyless neoliberal banker has been elected President of France, Donald Trump is an evil mastermind or a Russian operative, depending on what day it is (as opposed to just a completely incompetent, narcissistic billionaire idiot), and neoliberal propaganda outfits like *The New York Times*, *The Washington Post*, MSNBC, CNN, *The Guardian*, NPR, et al., are perceived as "respectable" sources of journalism, as if their role in generating and occasionally revising the official narrative weren't so insultingly obvious.

Personally, I am looking forward to the upcoming German elections this autumn, wherein Neoliberal Party "A" will be challenging Neoliberal Party "B" for the right to continue privatizing Greece (and any other formerly sovereign nations the transnational banks can get their hands on) in a demonstration of European unity, and fiscal austerity … and, you know, whatever.

If this is the Death of Neoliberalism, just imagine what awaits us at the Resurrection.

The Good Americans

June 2, 2017

The Pink Revolution of 2017, better known as Russiagate, is now more or less a *fait accompli*. Whether the corporatist ruling classes and their servants in Congress formally impeach him or force him to resign in disgrace, Donald J. Trump is being regime-changed, or at the very least effectively neutralized until he can be replaced with a grown-up, i.e., someone who will serve their interests without getting the masses all riled up about "taking the government back from the elites," putting "America first," and ... well, just generally making an ass of himself.

At this point, not even a war will save him. Even if he could somehow manage to convince the boys in the Pentagon to back an invasion of Iran, or Syria, or wherever, the corporate-owned media would crucify him, and you can't arbitrarily invade other countries without the support of the corporate media. No, the simple fact is, the Corporatocracy has decided to make an example of Trump, to remind folks who is really running things, and what happens when you attempt to defy them, and there's nothing Trump can do about it, other than rant and rave on Twitter.

The United States of America being a profoundly authoritarian society (whose citizens have been conditioned from childhood to follow orders, go through channels, submit to a host of humiliating rituals devised by an ever-expanding range of government and private "security services," and to worship leaders, police, soldiers, and, basically, anyone wearing a uniform, or a Giorgio Armani business suit), this ruling class soft coup is cause for celebration. Good Americans up and down both coasts are already dusting off their vuvuzelas. It isn't quite time to use them yet, but they want to be ready for the moment Trump waddles across the lawn of the White House, boards Marine One for the final time, and is flown away to exile in Florida, or to Leavenworth to be hanged for treason. At which point they, these Good Americans, will pour en masse onto

Lafayette Square, hooting, hollering, and waving flags, as they did when Obama sent Seal Team Six to roust the former CIA asset, Osama bin Laden, out of bed, shoot him several times in the face, and then dump his body in the Indian Ocean, or whatever it was that actually happened.

Good Americans, as a general rule, are not overly concerned with what actually happened. Or what is actually happening now. Or at least they're not too concerned with the details. History, politics, economics, not to mention the inner workings of the media, are complicated subjects best left to experts. Good Americans trust such experts (not implicitly, they're not dupes, after all) to explain what happened, or what is happening, to them. They have no choice but to trust these experts, and government officials, and the mainstream media, and the general consensus among the members of their privileged socioeconomic circles, as they do not have the time or the energy to go digging through reams of declassified documents, or to check the facts of the stories that appear in *The New York Times* or *The Washington Post*, or on their National Public Radio affiliate, or to read a book about history or politics, or the dissemination of propaganda written by someone who isn't parroting the official narrative of the ruling classes. What with all the demands of work, family, Facebook, Twitter, yoga, shopping, keeping up-to-date with the latest dining trends, not to mention the new season of *House of Cards*, there simply aren't enough hours in the day to scrutinize everything their leaders are doing, or the "information" the media is feeding them.

This does not make these Good Americans accomplices to any alleged atrocities perpetrated by their elected government. The United States isn't Nazi Germany. OK, sure, we wiped out the Native Americans (and sadistically named some of our sports teams after them), but that was hundreds of years ago. The same goes for slavery ... ancient history. And, all right, so the United States, and the indigenous death squads we have trained and funded, have murdered millions of men, women, and children in places like Indochina, Indonesia, Central America, South America, and the Middle East, and we've bombed and invaded a long list of countries that posed no threat to us whatsoever purely to advance the interests of the corporations that own the government, and their ongoing quest for global hegemony … still, it's not like Nazi Germany, where people went blithely on with their lives, pretending they had no idea what was happening.

No, these Good Americans, who at the moment are shrieking for Donald Trump's head on a pike because the CIA and the corporate-owned media told them he's a Russian operative, or that the Russians somehow "hacked" the election, are not at all like the Germans back then. Parroting the mindless propaganda pumped out by a global network of corporate media that Joseph Goebbels would have given Hitler's other nut to control, and otherwise collaborating with the intelligence agencies, financial elites, and other deep-state players intent on making an example of Trump, is … OK, admittedly, pretty pathetic, but it's not like looking the other way while your government methodically kills the Jews. On top of which, Trump really is a bad guy, and Good Americans traditionally support, or at least don't raise a major fuss about, the summary removal of government leaders the mainstream media tells them are bad guys.

Coincidentally, a lot of these bad guys, in addition to being hideously evil, have been, circa the time of their removal, interfering with the vital interests of the corporations that own our government. Bashar al-Assad, Muammar Gaddafi, and Saddam Hussein are the most recent examples, but we've been doing this since the late 1940s. A partial list of CIA ops, including, but not limited to, assassinations, torture, election rigging, fomenting coups, training death squads, and so on, stretching back to the post-WWII period, when we re-installed fascists in Greece and Italy and smuggled Nazis like Reinhard Gehlen, Klaus Barbie (a/k/a "the Butcher of Lyon"), and Eichmann's good buddy, Otto von Bolschwing, to America to help us defeat "the Communists," is available for perusal online, and in any number of books and articles.[1] It's not like this stuff is secret or anything.

But whatever ... no government is perfect, right? And the Good Americans are grown-ups, after all. So they understand that all that crap about democracy is important to teach the children, and to put on the masthead of your newspaper, or whatever, but the real world

1 Kangas, Steve, "A Timeline of CIA Atrocities," Global Research News, June 9, 1997

doesn't work like that.

In the real world, where the Good Americans live, safely insulated from the abject poverty they are not in any way responsible for creating, sometimes you have to hire a few Nazis, or support a couple of fascist regimes, or sell a few buttloads of arms to the Saudis, despite the fact that they're a brutal theocracy and the primary sponsors of the terrorism we claim to be bombing the Middle East to stop, or bankrupt a few hundred thousand Americans to bail out your pals at the Wall Street banks that bled them dry with their Ponzi scheme, or support an apartheid state like Israel, or sell Americans some convoluted corporate-friendly healthcare plan as if it were somehow completely impossible to provide a universal healthcare system like every other developed country, or lead the world in mass incarceration, primarily of the lower classes, who are already mass incarcerated in ghettos patrolled by militarized police, which of course bears no resemblance at all to the ghettos in Nazi-occupied Europe, and is regrettably just a permanent feature of the grown-up reality the Good Americans are utterly powerless to ever change.

All right, I know you're probably thinking that sounds a lot like the rationalizations the Good Germans used to excuse themselves for not resisting the horrors of the Nazis, but it isn't the same kind of thing at all. The Good Americans *are* resisting … they're resisting Trump, who, after all, is the one responsible for all that stuff, all those wars of aggression, the CIA coups, the torture, the death squads, the ghettos, et cetera … our entire seventy-two-year history as enforcer of global capitalist empire and all the incalculable human suffering and irreparable damage to the planet it has caused … all that is somehow the doing of Trump and his puppet-master, Vladimir Putin. Or at least it's not Obama's fault, or the fault of any of his Democrat predecessors, those champions of the poor and downtrodden who never needed to be resisted.

So please join the Good Americans this weekend as they do their part to help the corporatist establishment make an example of this monster (whose evil outstrips that of Hitler, and Pol Pot, and Stalin, and ... well, pick your monster) and discourage any future billionaire ass hats from screwing with their simulation of democracy.

They'll be staging huge rallies all around the country to whip up support for the Pink Revolution, and possibly even all-out nuclear blitzkrieg against our bestial Slavic enemies before they "influence" another election, or hack another rural power grid. They're calling it the March for Truth. It's a totally grassroots volunteer effort that has absolutely nothing to do with David Brock, Peter Daou, Shareblue Media,[2] the Democratic Party, or any of their neoliberal backers.

This one probably won't quite match the Nuremberg rallies for flat-out hysteria, but give the ruling classes some time … "Resistance Summer" is just getting started.[3]

---

2 McElrath, Leah, "More than 70 cities will "March for Truth" to demand independent Russian probe," Shareblue Media, May 15, 2017

3 Kamisar, Ben, "Dems launch 'Resistance Summer'," The Hill, May 16, 2017

The De-Putin-Nazification of America

August 11, 2017

Sometime circa late July, as the hundreds of thousands of de facto vassals that cater to the needs of New York City's simulated aristocracy were navigating the sweltering hell that the subway system has recently become, approximately one hundred miles to the east, deep in the heart of Resistance territory, where villas rent for up to a million a month, members of the notorious Bridgehampton Cell of the Neoliberal Liberation Army were gathered in one of their luxury safehouses, vetting the latest leading candidate for the coveted position of "resistance leader."

California Senator Kamala Harris, multimillionaire woman of the people, and friend of rapacious banks like OneWest,[1] must have impressed the Bridgehampton Cell, because their comrades in corporate media immediately launched a propaganda campaign to get the word out to the American people (who've been suffering under occupation for going on the last seven months) that the Senator and her affluent backers represent their last best hope of overthrowing the Trumpian Reich and saving the world from the Putin-Nazis.

For those unfamiliar with the Putin-Nazis, it's an official term I recently made up to describe, not just the Russian Federation, and Vladimir Putin and his inner circle, but also the maleficent global alliance of Russian hackers, Russian propagandists, Russian diplomats, Russian businesspersons, persons married to Russian persons, persons with Russian-sounding names, neo-Nazis, alt-Right geeks, Goldman Sachs guys, Sandernistas, Corbynistas, former coal miners, hillbilly oxycodone addicts, socialists, anarchists, Black Lives Matterists, the ghost of George Carlin, the ACLU, and anyone who has ever retweeted Wikileaks or didn't vote for Hillary Clinton.

---

1 Dayen, David, "Kamala Harris Fails to Explain Why She Didn't Prosecute Steven Mnuchin's Bank," The Intercept, January 5, 2017

As I'm sure you'll recall, the Putin-Nazis originally materialized out of thin air around the time that Clinton was managing to lose the U.S. presidential election to a repulsive, jabbering, narcissistic clown with absolutely no political experience, who the mainstream media had been assuring the world for months was the Second Coming of Hitler. Given that it was virtually impossible for Clinton to lose to such a noxious buffoon, the only rational explanation was that the Russians had somehow "hacked" the election, or "interfered with," or "influenced" the election. They had done this by getting their hands on a batch of internal Democratic Party emails, passing them on to Putin-Nazi Propaganda Minister Julian Assange, who published them on the Internet, where they were read by former Obama-voters, who were so completely shocked by their contents that they decided not to vote for Clinton, as they had obviously been intending to do, until their minds got "interfered with."

The rest, as they say, is history.

On January 20, despite the fact that everyone knew that the entire Trump family were Putin-Nazi "sleeper" agents, and that the man himself was the Glorious Leader of an underground army of neo-Nazis numbering in the tens of hundreds that was threatening the very fabric of democracy by circulating cartoon frogs on the Internet, Donald J. Trump was sworn in as President, and the Trumpian Reich officially began.

Fortunately, Americans are not a bunch of Camembert-slurping surrender monkeys. Although the ruling establishment was bound by law to allow a neo-fascist dictator who was clearly working for a hostile foreign power to move his circus into the White House, they were hardly going to sit idly by and watch as he transformed America into some sort of neo-nationalist dystopia where grade-school children would be forced to learn Russian, Hitler-salute the confederate flag, and whatever other Russo-Nazi horrors he and Bannon had in mind. Before Trump could even order the removal of every likeness of Martin Luther King from the D.C. metropolitan area, the Democratic Party, patriotic Republicans, the Intelligence Community, the corporate-owned media, and, of course, just millions of Good Americans launched a grassroots resistance movement to remove him from office by any means necessary.

Seven months later, here we are, with a Special Counsel and a D.C. grand jury, who will certainly be able to find something on Trump, or at least ensure that he spends the rest of his term denying the stream of allegations, rumors, and leaks that will flow therefrom.

Which means it's time to start getting ready for the day when our national nightmare is over, and Kamala Harris (or whichever loyal figurehead the ruling classes ultimately choose) marches through Washington like Charles de Gaulle, presumably with the Obamas and Clintons in tow, after which the U.S.A. can continue to bomb, occupy, sanction, and otherwise destabilize various other countries, allow its banks to debt-enslave its citizens, maintain a brutal, militarized police force, and everything else it's doing at the moment, but in a normal, liberal, non-fascist manner, and Stephen Colbert can get back to comedy.

Now, to pull this off, the Resistance is going to need to deal with all these Putin-Nazis, specifically the Putin-Nazis on the Left, who are already tweeting "fake news" tweets impugning the character of Senator Harris (who happens to be black, and a woman, by the way ... not that that has anything to do with anything), and reminding Americans how they got bamboozled by Obama's Hope-and-Change routine. These people need to be de-Putin-Nazified, and they need to be de-Putin-Nazified immediately. The last thing the Resistance needs at this point is to go through all the trouble of regime-changing Trump, only to have Americans elect some other non-vetted, narcissistic billionaire who thinks it might be fun to run for president.

This De-Putin-Nazification Program is going to involve a concerted effort on the part of the entire neoliberal establishment to stigmatize anyone who voted for Trump, or who didn't vote for Hillary Clinton, or who questions the integrity of Kamala Harris (who, as I may have already mentioned, is black), as a bug-eyed, Sieg-heiling Putin-Nazi. These people are going to need to be shamed, guilt-tripped, and otherwise emotionally manipulated into keeping their Putin-Nazi mouths shut. This isn't going to work on your actual fascists, but it will work on nearly everyone else, or at least on those Obama voters who didn't turn out for Hillary Clinton, and those bitter white Bernie Bros who voted for Trump as a personal "fuck you" to the Democratic Party.

See, odd as this is going to sound, the majority of your Putin-Nazis don't see themselves as Putin-Nazis. They see themselves ... well, as just regular Americans who have lost all faith in the electoral system, and who believe they are living in a sham republic controlled by global corporations and obscenely wealthy individuals who couldn't care less about them and their families, and whose only allegiance is to a transnational class of corporatist leeches like themselves. Still, despite their cynical beliefs, most of these folks are not particularly fond of being likened to Nazis, or racists, or xenophobes, or useful idiots. So this is exactly what the Resistance is doing, and intends to keep doing for the next few years (i.e., calling their detractors bad names, basically), so that any anti-corporatist dissent that they can't get Google to make disappear with an "anti-fake news algorithm" can be stigmatized as racist, misogynist, or some other variation of "deplorable."

Now, they need our help to make this work. Don't worry about the Russia hysteria. The corporate-owned media will take care of that. You want to focus on the fascism aspect, and the racism, misogyny, and xenophobia stuff, which is always the best way to silence other leftists.

Here are a few simple things you can do.

(1) Exaggerate the neo-fascist threat! You can do this on Twitter and Facebook endlessly. Forget about the fact that the number of actual fascists in America is ridiculously small, and that odds of some sort of fascist takeover of the U.S. government are infinitesimal. Convince your friends and Twitter followers that the fascists are on the verge of launching a national fascist revolution. Tweet about their "leaders" as if they were actual players on the national political stage, and not just a handful of pathetic creeps parading around in their Hitler hairdos for two or three hundred other such creeps. The point here is to help the Resistance keep folks' attention focused on "the fascists," and the racists, misogynists, xenophobes, et al., and not on the global capitalist elites and the vast transnational corporations that currently control most Western governments.

(2) Hammer the identity politics! Do not miss an opportunity to call out anyone who accidentally writes, speaks, or otherwise dis-

seminates a word or phrase that oppresses anyone, or that displays any type of unacknowledged privilege. Not only will this help the Resistance keep folks divided into an ever-increasing number of powerless little sub-groups that pose no threat to the corporatist ruling classes, it will feel really good to self-righteously hector anyone whose values are different from yours, especially members of the working classes who couldn't afford to go to university and learn about intersectionality, and so on. These folks are virtually fascists anyway. What difference does it make if you alienate them?

(3) Now, this one is absolutely crucial. Keep comparing Trump to Hitler! If you don't have time for the other two, at least you can help the Resistance with this one. See, it's really important that folks believe that Trump is not just a random bozo who rode a wave of populist anger and distrust of the Democrats into the White House, and who is now in the process of being neutralized by the people who actually run the country. He needs to be seen as a powerful dictator, who at any moment is liable to start … well, you know, killing the Jews, or something. Plus, this dovetails with the other two points. Exaggerating the fascist threat works much better when you have a powerful Hitler figure you can wag your finger at. And, given that Trump is actually a bigot, and a misogynist pig, and a xenophobe (or at least he plays one on TV), you can have a field day with the identity politics. So go hard on the Hitler stuff, and any kind of German references you can think of. Spell his name "Drumpf," or call him "Herr Trump," or put a little Hitler-mustache on him. Don't worry about getting chastised by any intersectionalist purity freaks. These kinds of slurs are perfectly acceptable, because, as every Good American knows, the Germans are, and will always be, Nazis.

These are just a few ideas to get started with. I'm sure you can think up some more on your own. The main thing is to steer well clear of any kind of political analysis that reminds folks about that corporatocracy, or how much it costs to get elected to office, and where the majority of that money comes from, and thus how irrelevant electoral politics is.

Oh, and keep an eye out for those Putin-Nazis! You never know where they're going to turn up, and I'd hate to see your mind get "interfered" with.

A De-Putin-Nazification of America Update

August 18, 2017

So, the De-Putin-Nazification of America couldn't be going much better at the moment. In terms of emotionally manipulating people (and especially any heretofore wayward members of the American "Left") into forming a mindless, hysterical mob and running around like headless chickens branding anyone who didn't vote for Hillary Clinton a goose-stepping Nazi, this past week has been a huge success. At this point, if you haven't posted an anti-Nazi loyalty oath on Twitter, Facebook, or some other platform, you're a potential "Nazi sympathizer" ... and you don't want to be one of those, now do you?

No, I didn't think you did. So, if you haven't done that, you'd better get on it. Here are few tips to get you started.

Your anti-Nazi loyalty oath should include a clearly-worded statement acknowledging that Donald Trump is Hitler, or at least the leader of the tens of hundreds of imbecilic, neo-Nazi losers who, according to most of the mainstream media, are on the verge of overthrowing the entire American ruling establishment. It should also include a threat to unfollow, de-friend, and otherwise socially ostracize anyone who hasn't posted such an oath, or who, despite the Charlottesville Kristallnacht, stubbornly continues thinking critically, or maintains any form of historical awareness, or presents any kind of rational arguments challenging the prevailing Nazi hysteria.

It should also include one or more of the following:

(1) If not an outright call for the First Amendment to be repealed, then at least a demand for a ban on "hate speech," and the removal of every hate-based statue, flag, painting, book, film, song, joke, or other expression of racism, hatred, religious bigotry, misogyny, extremism, general rudeness, and any other forms of speech or expression that you don't like, from public view. Don't worry about the ramifications of this ban. It will never, ever, be used against you, or anyone that

you agree with, or against any authors or artists that you like. It'll be a ban on "hate-speech," after all, and it's not like that term is completely subjective, or subject to the arbitrary whims of those in power, or anything like that.

(2) A demand that the already overly-broad definition of "terrorism" now be expanded even further, to include the fascist who drove his car into a crowd of counterprotesters in Charlottesville, killing one and wounding many others. Never mind that this murderous idiot seems to have done this on the spur of the moment (or, if it *was* a planned attack, that he's even more of an idiot than he seems, which, judging from his mug shot, is hard to believe). The important thing is to help the Resistance expand the definition of "terrorism" to the point where they can slap it onto anyone. Again, don't worry about the ramifications. The "terrorist" label will never, ever, be used against groups that you approve of, or innocent people in faraway countries that some future president wants to murder with drones. The Resistance would never, ever, do that. They know who is and who isn't a terrorist. And if they don't, they can always check with Obama.

(3) A reference (either veiled or direct) to someone who may be a Nazi-sympathizer. This is crucial in terms of motivating others to post their loyalty oaths, and fostering an atmosphere of paranoia, which is always so helpful at times like this. Surely, you know of someone who has said, tweeted, published, or posted something that could be interpreted as "Nazi-friendly." Don't bother with the Trump supporters. The corporate-owned media will take care of them. You want to go after other Leftists, specifically leftists who have been reluctant to call Trump Hitler, or a Putinist agent, or who disagree with you about Syria, or ... you know, just people who get on your nerves. This is a golden opportunity to pore through their tweets and Facebook posts, find something you can use against them, and then accuse them of harboring Nazi sympathies. Given the current level of hysteria, few people are going to check your facts. This is one you can really have fun with. See how far you can push the paranoia. Make up elaborate conspiracy theories. If you're not quite sure how to go about that, check *The New York Times* or *The Washington Post* ... they're masters of that kind of thing.

Your anti-Nazi loyalty oath should definitely *not* include any of the following:

(1) Any mention of the Ukrainian Nazis that Obama, Clinton, and the rest of the Resistance (before it was the Resistance, of course) helped regime-change the Ukrainian government when it wouldn't play ball with the EU and NATO. Mentioning the Resistance's support of these Nazis would only confuse those reading your oath, who might not understand that there are good Nazis and bad Nazis, and who have probably forgotten how the U.S. government smuggled a number of actual Nazis (i.e., members of the NSDAP) into America after WWII … or how, since the end of that war, the United States has mass-murdered countless millions of people all over the planet (but, technically, not in a genocidal fashion, so that doesn't make us the same as Nazis).

(2) Actual membership figures on neo-Nazi and white supremacist groups, because those figures are pathetically small. Doing this would make your loyalty oath (not to mention the whole Nazi hysteria thing, generally) seem, if not paranoid, then at least absurd, or like part of some manufactured effort to whip up support for a ruling class coup by waving Nazis in front of everyone's faces. This would be extremely counterproductive. Remember, one of the primary goals of the De-Putin-Nazification program is to convince the public that Richard Spencer (and the handful of other insignificant idiots that the corporate media is showering with publicity) is about to lead an overwhelming force of tiki torch-bearing neo-Nazis into the streets of American cities to battle the hyper-militarized police, the national guard, and the U.S. military, or some other preposterous scenario like that.

(3) Any reference whatsoever to the corporatocracy that runs the country, and that normally decides who can run for president, and which is currently making an example of Trump in order to dissuade any future billionaires from having the audacity to fuck with them. You'll be better off avoiding this subject entirely, as it only reminds folks how screwed they are, and how, odds are, they're probably all worked up about something the corporate-owned media wanted to get them all worked up about: neo-Nazis, Russian hackers, nuclear war with North Korea, Syrian gas attacks, lone wolf terrorists, weap-

ons of mass destruction, or whatever. Take it from someone who's worked in show business. No one likes being made aware of how they are being emotionally manipulated ... or provided with a binary set of officially acceptable contextual parameters within which they can think and speak.

But don't worry too much about that binary stuff. There'll be plenty of time to get into all that after we rid the world of these Nazis, and these racists, and all these Confederate statues. And Trump, of course. That's the main thing ... getting rid of Donald Trump, and getting a Democrat back in office. Oh, yeah ... and the books. We need to look at the books. God knows how many Confederate books are still out there in the public libraries, and in people's homes, where children can read them. We'll need to get to the books eventually.

In the meantime, focus on Priority One. Go hard on the Nazi hysteria, at least throughout the rest of the weekend, after which they'll probably need to switch us back to the Russia hysteria, or possibly the North Korea hysteria, or ... damn, see? Here I go with that contextual parameter stuff again. I've really got to stop doing that. The last thing I need is to get myself accused of being some kind of Nazi sympathizer, or Confederate apologist, or Russian propagandist, or extremist, or terrorist, or, you know ... whatever.

The United States of Manufactured Hysteria

September 1, 2017

Thank God for the Charlottesville Nazis! For a moment there, it was looking like we were actually going to have a few days to stop and reflect on the state of America without being subjected to some new form of manufactured mass hysteria. Seriously, just a few short weeks ago, as the corporatist ruling classes' ridiculous attempt to convince the world that Donald Trump is some sort of Russian sleeper agent appeared to be finally fizzling out,[1] a significant number of leftist types were beginning to wonder if maybe, just maybe, the fact that the United States government is controlled by a global corporate plutocracy that has no allegiance to any nation, or people, or to anything other than itself, and that is in the process of demonizing and potentially deposing an elected president … that maybe that might be something to focus on, not exclusively, by any means, but alongside other vital issues, like defending the rights of transgender drone pilots and purging syllabi of oppressive pronouns.

Fortunately, thanks to the Nazis of Charlottesville, this dangerous moment of doubt has now passed. If you were listening closely on August 11, you could hear the collective sigh of relief whooshing out of Resistance quarters like a hypnagogic idiot wind as roughly one hundred white supremacists marched into town with their tiki torches barking out NSDAP slogans and otherwise making asses of themselves.

Corporate media apparatchiks, mandarins of the Internet Left, professional and amateur Naziologists, and assorted other Nazi experts immediately went to DEFCON 1, signaling imminent Nazi invasion. Photos of bug-eyed, torch-bearing Nazis, their mouths wide open in mid-Nazi shriek, veins bulging out of their Nazi

---

1 Lawrence, Patrick, "A New Report Raises Big Questions About Last Year's DNC Hack," The Nation, August 9, 2017

necks, were released to the public and circulated widely. Millions of conflicted leftists (many of whom had been feeling uneasy about collaborating with the corporate plutocracy in their efforts to delegitimize Trump, and every last American who voted for him), upon seeing glossy color close-ups of these Nazis waved in front of their faces, responded as every Good American has been conditioned to respond since early childhood. They instantly switched off their critical faculties and began reenacting the Second World War … or rather, the mythical version of it wherein the U.S.A. defeated the Nazis, which is one of Americans' favorite pastimes.

Look, I don't mean to make light of Charlottesville. We're talking actual neo-Nazis, with actual Nazi flags and haircuts, shouting actual Nazi slogans, and the Ku Klux Klan, and heavily-armed militia, and just garden variety racist rednecks … all of which have been standard features of American life for decades,[2] and longer,[3] but this is no time to reflect on history, or try to put things into perspective.

Also, one of these Nazi morons ran over people with his car the next day, killing one woman, and injuring many others, which renders any critical thinking about the actual size of the Nazi menace (which remains ridiculously small, as ever) or the motives of the corporate media in blowing it up all out of proportion tantamount to Nazi sympathizing, and I'm already in enough trouble as it is.

Plus, Charlottesville was just the beginning … kind of like a Nazi Tet Offensive. Just one week later, on August 19, literally forty to fifty Nazis (cleverly disguised as Trump supporters, libertarians, and right-wing oddballs) occupied a public gazebo in Boston,[4] and were right on the verge of expressing virulent Nazi views to the riot cops surrounding them. Luckily, just in the nick of time, a contingent of approximately forty thousand anti-fascist Resistance members arrived on the scene to deny them a platform, and chase down anyone wearing one of those MAGA hats and verbally abuse them.

You'd think the Nazis would have gotten the message … but no,

2 Beckett, Lois, "George Lincoln Rockwell, father of American Nazis, still in vogue for some," The Guardian, August 27, 2017

3 Weeks, Linton, "When The KKK Was Mainstream," National Public Radio, March 19, 2015

4 Staff, "Boston 'free speech' rally ends after counter-protesters take to streets," CBS News, August 19, 2017 (https://www.cbsnews.com/news/boston-free-speech-rally-thousands-take-to-the-streets-in-rival-protests-live-updates/)

last Sunday, August 27, another ten or eleven Nazis (many of them posing as Trump supporters, as if that didn't make them Nazis, and some of them even going so far as to attempt to pass themselves off as "Latinos") audaciously tried to assemble in Berkeley.

The Resistance showed them no mercy this time. Thousands of peaceful counter-protesters quickly frightened the Nazis away, and then squads of masked-up anti-fascists hunted down any Nazi-looking stragglers, "apparent alt-righters," and nosy photographers, and stomped the living Hitler out of them.

This preemptive, self-defensive stomping alarmed the more liberal wing of the Resistance, so they set about branding the anti-fascists who had beaten the crap out of the people the liberals had branded Nazis "domestic terrorists."

Elsewhere in America, Resistance members were frantically tearing down Confederate monuments,[5] which had suddenly become intolerably offensive, and searching through online business directories for anyone named after Robert E. Lee, or horses named after General Lee's horse,[6] or the horses of other racist Nazis. That, and hastily organizing the upcoming "March to Confront White Supremacy" (presumably in order to make a mockery of the 1963 March on Washington), and penning lengthy explications of the evils of racism, white supremacy, and any and all other forms of Nazism associated with Donald Trump ... and otherwise whipping people up into a sputtering frenzy of Nazi hysteria.

Now, you have to hand it to the fake Resistance. This Nazi hysteria is good for everyone. Not only is it an easier sell than that ridiculous Russian hacking nonsense (because Trump really is a racist, of course), but it's something the broader Left can embrace, as it plugs straight into identity politics, which is pretty much all we've got these days.

See, up to now, the dilemma we've been facing (or some of us have been facing, anyway) is how to respond to the ruling establishment's concerted campaign to "regime-change" Trump. On the one hand,

---

5 Associated Press, "Confederate statue toppled in North Carolina during anti-racism rally," The Guardian, August 15, 2017

6 Fenno, Nathan, "Traveler, USC's mascot, comes under scrutiny for having a name similar to Robert E. Lee's horse," Los Angeles Times, August 18, 2017

Trump is a living embodiment of everything the Left opposes. On the other hand, going after Trump has meant carrying water for the fake Resistance, i.e., that global corporatocracy (which, by the way, does not mean "the Jews" ... I always like to slip that in to piss off my anti-Semitic readers).

This has been a bit awkward for some of us, i.e., restraining our impulse to stick it to Trump (at least on whatever talking points the Resistance is currently putting out) because in doing so we would align ourselves with the ruling establishment's attempt to demonize and eventually depose an American president who isn't playing ball with them properly. If we oppose regime change in other countries, shouldn't we also oppose it at home? Or do the ruling classes get a pass this time because Trump is such an exceptional monster? But wait ... wasn't Saddam a monster? And Gaddafi? And all the other "Hitlers" that wouldn't play ball with the corporatocracy? And Assad? Isn't he a monster?

You can see how confusing all this gets, when you're trying to figure out how to oppose both the supranational corporatocracy that is superseding sovereign nations as the hegemonic power in the world and the neo-nationalist reaction against it, which *is*, essentially, fascist in nature, and which the corporatocracy also opposes, and desperately wants you to help them oppose by buying their manufactured hysteria about Russians, or Nazis, or whatever scary monster they wave in front of your face. After a while, your brain starts to hurt, and you just want someone to make things simple.

Charlottesville Nazis to the rescue! How much simpler could it get? Corporatocracy? What corporatocracy? We got goddamned Nazis coming out of the woodwork! Racist Nazis! Confederate Nazis! Nazi apologists! Nazi sympathizers! This is no time to worry about who's actually wielding political power, or how they're manufacturing hysteria and otherwise emotionally manipulating people (not you, of course ... other people). No, what we need to do now is censor the Internet,[7] and any other venues for Nazi "hate speech," and round up all these racist Nazis and subject them to anti-Nazi

7 Bergen, Mark, "Google begins biggest ever crackdown on extremist YouTube videos," The Independent, August 25, 2017

therapy, or anti-racist empathy programs,[8] or just gang up on them and beat them senseless.

OK, sure, that might sound extreme, or authoritarian, or just plain old creepy, but keep in mind that This Is Not Normal! And racism and Nazism is very, very bad. And Love Trumps Hate! And Scope Kills Germs! And we never literally meant that Trump was an actual Russian agent or anything. Forget about all that Russia stuff now. Trump is Hitler. Trump has always been Hitler. America has always been at war with Hitler. America will always be at war with Hitler.

Oh, yeah, and I almost forgot, today's edition of the Two Minutes Hate will begin in approximately fifteen minutes. Please assemble in the usual location. Thank you for your cooperation.

---

8 Street, Paul, "The Road to Charlottesville: Reflections on 21st Century U.S. Capitalist Racism," CounterPunch, August 25, 2017

The Ever More Orwellian Definition of Terrorism

October 6, 2017

In terms of twisting the English language into a ludicrous Orwellian mockery of itself in order to short-circuit critical thinking, this has been a particularly good week. My favorite part so far has been the part where respectable leftists writers have been arguing that the already arbitrary application of the label "terrorist" should now be rendered even more arbitrary. I'm not talking about establishment liberals in corporatist papers like *The New York Times*. I'm talking about writers I generally respect, and fearless, adversarial outlets like *The Intercept* and *CounterPunch*.

For example, in his essay on Wednesday, "The NRA's Latest Terrorist Attack on U.S. Soil,"[1] Paul Street argues that the "terrorist" label should be applied, not just to the Las Vegas shooter,[2] but also to the NRA. Here, I believe, is the crux of his argument:

> "I am aware that the formal definition of terrorism involves the use of violence to achieve a political objective – a ruthless means to political ends. Does the actual shooter have to be a member of the terrorist organization – in this case, by my analysis, the NRA – and on board with its agenda? No, not when it comes to advancing the NRA's political goals. All that's required is that he kills a lot of people."

This, of course, is the very same logic employed by the media and

1 Street, Paul, "The NRA's Latest Terrorist Attack on U.S. Soil," CounterPunch, October 4, 2017

2 On October 1, 2017, Stephen Paddock opened fire from the 32nd floor of the Mandalay Bay Hotel and Casino, firing into a crowd of people attending a concert on the Las Vegas strip, killing 58 and wounding 851. Paddock, whose motives remain unknown, had stocked his suite with an arsenal of over 20 semi-automatic rifles, many of which he had converted to fully-automatic with so-called "bump stocks."

the "intelligence community" when they label any mass-murdering psycho who claims to be part of some terrorist group that he has never had any contact with a "suddenly self-radicalized terrorist." These would be folks like Omar Mateen, Mohamed Salmene Lahouaiej-Bouhlel, Khalid Masood, and assorted other killers, who I have personally designated "non-terrorist terrorists,"[3] due to the inconvenient fact that they appear to have had no connection to terrorism prior to deciding to kill a lot of people. But whatever ... according to Paul Street's logic, and the logic of the "intelligence community," a person doesn't need to be a member of any actual terrorist group, or be otherwise connected to terrorism, to be officially designated a "terrorist."

And if that kind of reasoning seems less than convincing, Binoy Kampmark, in his Wednesday essay, "What's in a Word? Terrorism in Las Vegas,"[4] offers the following justification for deeming the Las Vegas perpetrator a "terrorist":

> "The Nevada statute should have provided ample guidance to the authorities about what had transpired: 'an act of terrorism means any act that involves the use or attempted use of sabotage, coercion or violence which is intended to cause great bodily harm or death to the general population.' Down pat, precise, unquestionable."

Well, gosh, if the legislature of the State of Nevada has passed a law enabling the authorities to designate any mass murderer a "terrorist," I guess that should be good enough for us. Who can argue with the law, after all? Let's all just pray that the Nevada legislature doesn't declare some activist group that we happen to support "domestic terrorists" because they're trying to "coerce the general population" by causing "bodily harm" to someone.

And it's not just my fellow *CounterPunch* contributors who've been going, shall we say, a little overboard. Tim Dickenson, in *Rolling*

3 "The Dawning of the Age of Non-Terrorist Terrorism," CounterPunch, August 1, 2016

4 Kampmark, Binoy, "What's in a Word? Terrorism in Las Vegas," CounterPunch, October 4, 2017

Stone,[5] reiterates Street and Kampmark's arguments, or they reiterate his, or something. Shaun King, in a piece in *The Intercept*,[6] treats the subject with a bit more nuance, but the impression we are left with is basically the same; if not for the fact that the Las Vegas shooter was white, he would have been deemed a "terrorist." Which is true, of course, but beside the point.

While I appreciate these writers' frustration with the biased application of the "terrorist" label, helping the intelligence community expand the definition of "terrorist" to the point where they can just slap it onto anyone seems a bit reckless and … well, not so intelligent. It's kind of like arguing that because the police have been killing unarmed African Americans, the thing to do is demand that they also start killing unarmed white Americans, you know, just to keep things fair.

Call me what you want, but this isn't an argument I can enthusiastically get behind. Apart from the blatant absurdity of it, and the naked authoritarianism of it, there's also this hang-up I have with words, i.e., how I want them to actually mean things.

Emotionally loaded terms like "terrorism" don't mean anything. Their value is strategic. They are labels used by the ruling classes to designate violence that they haven't sanctioned. When Trump, or Obama, orders a drone to bomb some wedding party in Afghanistan and vaporizes an entire family, or when the IDF kills another kid for throwing rocks at a wall or something, this violence does not qualify as terrorism. On the other hand, if some Muslim individual, for whatever personal or "political" reasons,[7] decides to mass murder a lot of people and glorify his murder/suicide by claiming he is doing it for ISIS … well, sure, that definitely qualifies as terrorism. And when the mother of some other idiot who goes to Syria to join the terrorists the CIA is helping try to overthrow the Syrian govern-

---

5 Dickenson, Tim, "It's Time to Politicize the Terror Attack in Las Vegas," Rolling Stone, October 2, 2017

6 King, Shawn, "The White Privilege of the "Lone Wolf" Shooter," The Intercept, October 3, 2017

7 Hennessy-Fiske, Molly, Jarvie, Jenny, and Quentin Wilber, Del, "Orlando gunman had used gay dating app and visited LGBT nightclub on other occasions, witnesses say," Los Angeles Times, June 13, 2016; Greenwald, Glenn and Hussein, Murtaza, "As the Trial of Omar Mateen's Wife Begins, New Evidence Undermines Beliefs About the Pulse Massacre, Including Motive," The Intercept, March 5, 2018

ment wires her son a couple thousand Euros, she is sent to prison for "financing terrorism."[8]

And then there's the current corporate effort to eliminate "extremist" views on the Internet, and the intelligence agencies' classification of Antifa as "domestic terrorists."[9] These are just some of the many examples of how the ruling classes are using these terms (i.e, "terrorism," "extremism," etc.) to demonize anyone they want to demonize, and keep people living in a state of fear, so that they have no time for critical thinking, which is what these terms are designed to do.

And now, in response to the Las Vegas massacre, leftists are demanding that the perpetrator, Stephen Paddock, be labeled a "terrorist," because he furthers the NRA's political goals, or simply because he shot a lot of people.

Well, sure, I mean, why the hell not? If we leftists can argue that violence isn't violence, because it's preemptive self-defense against Nazis, whose speech is violence because they're Nazis, we can probably get away with this one. And heck, why should we stop with Paddock? Couldn't we, employing the same sort of logic, argue that every NRA member, and anyone who voted for Trump (who, after all, is a white supremacist and thus a "terrorist" by definition) … that all these people are also terrorists? Maybe, if we got enough Facebook likes, we could write to the Homeland Security folks and demand that they start up another terrorist database, or otherwise monitor these people's behavior.

Or maybe I'm just over-reacting and criticizing my fellow leftists unjustly. It probably doesn't really matter what words like "terrorist" actually mean, or what kind of authoritarian sentiment or convoluted Orwellian logic we promote in our alternative left-wing essays. By the time that Google and Facebook get finished cleansing the Internet of "extremist content," and every other type of content they have demonized with some meaningless label designed to shut off critical thinking and appeal to people's raw emotions, no one will be reading us anyway, except for the terrorists and extremists, of course.

---

8 Jarry, Emmanuel, "French court jails woman who sent money to son killed in Syria," Reuters, September 28, 2017

9 Pasha-Robinson, Lucy, "Antifa: US security agencies label group 'domestic terrorists'," The Independent, September 4, 2017

Tomorrow Belongs to the Corporatocracy

October 20, 2017

Back in October 2016, I wrote a somewhat divisive essay[1] in which I suggested that political dissent is being systematically pathologized. In fact, this process has been ongoing for decades, but it has been significantly accelerated since the Brexit referendum and the Rise of Trump (or, rather, the Fall of Hillary Clinton, as it was Americans' lack of enthusiasm for eight more years of corporatocracy with a sugar coating of identity politics, and not their enthusiasm for Trump, that mostly put the clown in office.)

In the twelve months since I wrote that piece, we have been subjected to a concerted campaign of corporate media propaganda for which there is no historical precedent. Virtually every major organ of the Western media apparatus (the most powerful propaganda machine in the annals of powerful propaganda machines) has been relentlessly churning out variations on a new official ideological narrative designed to generate and enforce conformity. The gist of this propaganda campaign is that "Western democracy" is under attack by a confederacy of Russians and white supremacists, as well as "the terrorists" and other "extremists" it's been under attack by for the last sixteen years.

I've been writing about this campaign for a year now, so I'm not going to rehash all the details. Suffice to say, we've gone from Russian operatives "hacking" the U.S. elections[2] to "Russia-linked" persons "apparently" setting up "illegitimate" Facebook accounts, "likely operated out of Russia," and publishing ads that are "indistinguishable from legitimate political speech" on the Internet.[3]

---

1 "The Pathologization of Dissent," CounterPunch, October 27, 2016

2 Maté, Aaron, "Russiagate is More Fiction than Fact," The Nation, October 6, 2017

3 Timberg, Craig, Dwoskin, Elizabeth, and Entous, Adam, "Obama tried to give Zuckerberg a wake-up call over fake news on Facebook," The Washington Post, September 24, 2017

This is what the corporate media are presenting as evidence of "an unprecedented foreign invasion of American democracy,"[4] a handful of political ads on Facebook.

In addition to the "Russian hacker" propaganda, since August, we have also been treated to relentless "white supremacist" hysteria.[5] The negligible American neo-Nazi subculture has been blown up into a biblical Behemoth inexorably slouching its way towards the White House lawn for the official launch of the Trumpian Reich.

At the same time, government and corporate entities have been aggressively restricting (and in many cases eliminating) fundamental civil liberties such as freedom of expression, freedom of the press, the right of assembly, the right to privacy, and the right to due process under the law. The justification for this curtailment of our rights (which started in earnest in 2001, following the September 11 attacks) is "protecting the public" from the threat of "terrorism."

As of now, the United States has been in a State of Emergency for over sixteen years.[6] The UK is in a virtual State of Emergency.[7] France is now in the process of enshrining its permanent State of Emergency into law.[8] Draconian counter-terrorism measures have been implemented throughout the EU.[9] Not only the notorious U.S. police[10] but police throughout the West have been militarized. Every other day we learn of some new "emergency security measure" designed to keep us safe from "the terrorists," the "lone wolf shooters," and other "extremists."[11]

Conveniently, since the Brexit referendum and unexpected election

---

4 The Editorial Board, "Russia's Fake Americans," The New York Times, September 8, 2017

5 Polakow-Suransky, Sasha, "White Nationalism Is Destroying the West," The New York Times, October 13, 2017

6 Korte, Gregory, "A permanent emergency: Trump becomes third president to renew extraordinary post-9/11 powers," USA Today, September 14, 2017

7 Dodd, Vikram, "UK facing most severe terror threat ever, warns MI5 chief," The Guardian, October 17, 2017

8 Rubin, Alissa J. and Peltier, Elian, "French Parliament Advances a Sweeping Counterterrorism Bill," The New York Times, October 4, 2017

9 Dalhuisen, John, "Warning: Europe is entering a permanent state of emergency," The Guardian, January 17, 2017

10 Greenwald, Glenn, "The Militarization of U.S. Police: Finally Dragged Into the Light by the Horrors of Ferguson," The Intercept, August 14, 2014

11 Murphy, Katharine, "Turnbull denies new facial recognition measures amount to 'mass surveillance'," The Guardian, October 5, 2017

of Trump (which is when the capitalist ruling classes first recognized that they had a widespread nationalist backlash on their hands), the definition of "terrorism" (or, more broadly, "extremism") has been expanded to include not just Al Qaeda, or ISIS, or whoever we're calling "the terrorists" these days, but anyone else the ruling classes decide they need to label "extremists." The FBI has designated Black Lives Matter "Black Identity Extremists."[12] The FBI and DHS have designated Antifa "domestic terrorists."[13] Hosting corporations have shut down several white supremacist and neo-Nazi websites,[14] along with their access to online fundraising. Google is algorithmically burying leftist news and opinion outlets like *Alternet*, *CounterPunch*, *Global Research*, *Consortium News*, and *Truthout*, among others.[15] Twitter, Facebook, and Google have teamed up to cleanse the Internet of "extremist content," "hate speech," and whatever else they arbitrarily decide is inappropriate.[16] YouTube, with assistance from the ADL (which deems pro-Palestinian activists and other critics of Israel "extremists") is censoring "extremist" and "controversial" videos, in an effort to "fight terrorist content online."[17] Facebook is also collaborating with Israel to thwart "extremism," "incitement of violence," and whatever else Israel decides is "inflammatory."[18] In the UK, simply reading "terrorist content" is punishable by fifteen years in prison.[19] Over three thousand people were arrested last year for publishing "offensive" and "menacing" material.[20]

---

12 Winter, Jana and Weinberger, Sharon, "The FBI's New U.S. Terrorist Threat: 'Black Identity Extremists'," Foreign Policy, October 6, 2017

13 Pasha-Robinson, Lucy, "Antifa: U.S. Security agencies label group 'domestic terrorists'," The Independent, September 4, 2017

14 Wong, Julia Carrie, "The far right is losing its ability to speak freely online. Should the left defend it?" The Guardian, August 28, 2017

15 Damon, Andre and Niemuth, Niles, "New Google algorithm restricts access to left-wing, progressive web sites," World Socialist Website, July 27, 2017

16 Solon, Olivia, "Facebook, Twitter, Google and Microsoft team up to tackle extremist content," The Guardian, December 6, 2016

17 Webb, Whitney, "Youtube moves to censor 'controversial' content, brings ADL on board as flagger," Mint Press News, August 7, 2017

18 Greenwald, Glenn, "Facebook Says It Is Deleting Accounts at the Direction of the U.S. and Israeli Governments," The Intercept, December 30, 2017

19 "Longer jail terms for viewing terror content online," BBC News, October 3, 2017

20 ""British police accused of 'wasting time' as hate speech arrests up almost 900% in some areas," RT, October 12, 2017

Whatever your opinion of these organizations and "extremist" persons is beside the point. I'm not a big fan of neo-Nazis, personally, but neither am I a fan of Antifa. I don't have much use for conspiracy theories, or a lot of the nonsense one finds on the Internet, but I consume a fair amount of alternative media, and I publish in *CounterPunch*, *The Unz Review*, *ColdType*, and other non-corporate journals. I consider myself a leftist, basically, but my political essays are often reposted by right-wing and, yes, even pro-Russia blogs. I get mail from former Sanders supporters, Trump supporters, anarchists, socialists, former 1960s radicals, anti-Semites, and other human beings, some of whom I passionately agree with, others of whom I passionately disagree with. As far as I can tell from the emails, none of these readers voted for Clinton, or Macron, or supported the TPP, or the debt-enslavement and looting of Greece, or the ongoing restructuring of the Greater Middle East (and all the lovely knock-on effects that has brought us), or believe that Trump is a Russian operative, or that Obama is Martin Luther Jesus-on-a-stick. What they share, despite their opposing views, is a general awareness that the locus of power in our post-Cold War age is primarily corporate, or global capitalist, and neoliberal in nature. They also recognize that they are being subjected to a massive propaganda campaign designed to lump them all together (again, despite their opposing views) into an intentionally vague and undefinable category comprising anyone and everyone, everywhere, opposing the hegemony of global capitalism, and its non-ideological ideology (the nature of which I'll get into in a moment).

As I wrote in that essay a year ago, "a line is being drawn in the ideological sand." This line cuts across both Left and Right, dividing what the capitalist ruling classes designate "normal" from what they label "extremist." The traditional ideological paradigm, Left versus Right, is disappearing (except as a kind of minstrel show), and is being replaced, or overwritten, by a pathological paradigm based upon the concept of "extremism."

Although the term has been around since the Fifth Century B.C., the concept of "extremism" as we know it today developed in the late

Twentieth Century and has come into vogue in the last three decades. During the Cold War, the official exonyms were "subversive," "radical," or just plain old "communist," all of which terms referred to an actual ideological adversary.

In the early 1990s, as the U.S.S.R. disintegrated, and globalized Western capitalism became the unopposed hegemonic ideological system that it is today, a new concept was needed to represent the official enemy and its ideology. The concept of "extremism" does that perfectly, as it connotes, not an external enemy with a definable ideological goal, but rather, a deviation from the norm. The nature of the deviation (e.g., right-wing, left-wing, faith-based, and so on) is secondary, almost incidental. The deviation itself is the point.

The "terrorist," the "extremist," the "white supremacist," the "religious fanatic," the "violent anarchist" … these figures are not rational actors whose ideas we need to intellectually engage with in order to debate or debunk. They are pathological deviations, mutant cells within the body of "normality," which we need to identify and eliminate, not for ideological reasons, but purely in order to maintain "security."

A truly global-hegemonic system like contemporary global capitalism (the first of this kind in human history), technically, has no ideology. "Normality" is its ideology … an ideology which erases itself and substitutes the concept of what is "normal," or, in other words, "just the way it is." The specific characteristics of "normality," although not quite arbitrary, are ever-changing. In the West, for example, thirty years ago, smoking was normal. Now, it's abnormal. Being gay was abnormal. Now, it's normal. Being transgender is becoming normal, although we're still in the early stages of the process. Racism has become abnormal. Body hair is currently abnormal. Walking down the street in a semi-fugue state robotically thumbing the screen of a smartphone that you just finished thumbing a minute ago is "normal." Capitalism has no qualms with these constant revisions to what is considered normal, because none of them are threats to capitalism. On the contrary, as far as values are concerned, the more flexible and commodifiable the better.

See, despite what intersectionalists will tell you, capitalism has no interest in racism, misogyny, homophobia, xenophobia, or any other despotic values (though it has no problem working with these values when they serve its broader strategic purposes). Capitalism is an economic system, which we have elevated to a social system. It only has one fundamental value, exchange value, which isn't much of a value, at least not in terms of organizing society or maintaining any sort of human culture or reverence for the natural world it exists in. In capitalist society, everything, everyone, every object and sentient being, every concept and human emotion, is worth exactly what the market will bear … no more, no less, than its market price.

There is no other measure of value.

Yes, we all want there to be other values, and we pretend there are, but there aren't, not really. Although we are free to enjoy parochial subcultures based on alternative values (i.e., religious bodies, the arts, and so on), these subcultures operate within capitalist society, and ultimately conform to its rules.

In the arts, for example, works are either commercial products, like any other commodity, or they are subsidized by what could be called "the simulated aristocracy," the Ivy League-educated leisure classes (and lower-class artists aspiring thereto) who need to pretend that they still have "culture" in order to feel superior to the masses. In the latter case, this feeling of superiority is the upscale product being sold. In the former, it is entertainment, distraction from the depressing realities of living, not in a society at all, but in a marketplace with no real human values. (In the absence of any actual cultural values, there is no qualitative difference between, say, Gerhard Richter and Adam Sandler. They're both successful capitalist artists. They're just selling their products in different markets.)

The fact that it has no human values is the evil genius of global capitalist society. Unlike the despotic societies it replaced, it has no allegiance to any cultural identities, traditions, or anything other than money. It can accommodate any form of government, as long as it plays ball with global capitalism. Thus, the window dressing of "normality" is markedly different from country to country, but the essence of "normality" remains the same. Even in countries with state religions, like Iran, or state ideologies, like China, the governments play by the rules of global capitalism like everyone else. If they don't, they can expect to receive a visit from global capitalism's

Regime Change Department (i.e., the U.S. military and its assorted partners).

Which is why, despite the "Russiagate" hysteria the media have been barraging us with, the West is not going to war with Russia. Nor are we going to war with China. Russia and China are developed countries, whose economies are entirely dependent on global capitalism, as are Western economies. The economies of every developed nation on the planet are inextricably linked. This is the nature of the global hegemony I've been referring to throughout this essay. Not American hegemony, but global capitalist hegemony. Systemic, supranational hegemony (which I prefer to call "the Corporatocracy," as it sounds more poetic and less post-structural).

We haven't really got our minds around it yet, because we're still in the early stages of it, but we have entered an epoch in which historical events are primarily being driven, and societies reshaped, not by sovereign nation states acting in their national interests but by supranational corporations acting in their corporate interests. Paramount among these corporate interests is the maintenance and expansion of global capitalism, and the elimination of any impediments thereto. Forget about the United States (i.e., the actual nation state) for a moment, and look at what's been happening since the early 1990s. The U.S. military's "disastrous misadventures" in Iraq, Libya, Afghanistan, Syria, and the former Yugoslavia, among other exotic places (which have obviously had nothing to do with the welfare or security of any actual Americans), begin to make a lot more sense.

Global capitalism, since the end of the Cold War (i.e., immediately after the end of the Cold War), has been conducting a global clean-up operation, eliminating actual and potential insurgencies, mostly in the Middle East, but also in its Western markets. Having won the last ideological war, like any other victorious force, it has been "clear-and-holding" the conquered territory, which in this case happens to be the whole planet.

Just for fun, get out a map, and look at the history of invasions, bombings, and other "interventions" conducted by the West and its assorted client states since 1990. Also, once you're done with that, consider how, over the last fifteen years, most Western societies have been militarized, their citizens placed under constant surveillance, and an overall atmosphere of "emergency" fostered, and paranoia about "the threat of extremism" propagated by the corporate media.

I'm not suggesting that there's a bunch of capitalists sitting around in a room somewhere in their shiny black top hats planning all of this. I'm talking about systemic development, which is a little more complex than that, and much more difficult to intelligently discuss because we're used to perceiving historico-political events in the context of competing nation states, rather than competing ideological systems ... or non-competing ideological systems, for capitalism has no competition. What it has, instead, is a variety of insurgencies, the faith-based Islamic fundamentalist insurgency and the neo-nationalist insurgency chief among them. There will certainly be others throughout the near future as global capitalism consolidates control and restructures societies according to its values.

None of these insurgencies will be successful.

Short some sort of cataclysm, like an asteroid strike or the zombie apocalypse, or, you know, violent revolution, global capitalism will continue to restructure the planet to conform to its ruthless interests. The world will become increasingly "normal." The scourge of "extremism" and "terrorism" will persist, as will the general atmosphere of "emergency." There will be no more Trumps, Brexit referendums, revolts against the banks, and so on. Identity politics will continue to flourish, providing a forum for leftist activist types (and others with an unhealthy interest in politics), who otherwise might become a nuisance, but any and all forms of actual dissent from global capitalist ideology will be systematically marginalized and pathologized.

This won't happen right away, of course. Things are liable to get ugly first (as if they weren't ugly enough already), but probably not in the way we're expecting, or being trained to expect by the corporate media. Look, I'll give you a dollar if it turns out I'm wrong, and the Russians, terrorists, white supremacists, and other "extremists" do bring down "democracy" and launch their Islamic, white supremacist, Russo-Nazi Reich, or whatever, but from where I sit it looks pretty clear ... tomorrow belongs to the Corporatocracy.

Who's Afraid of Corporate COINTELPRO?

November 3, 2017

On November 30, 2016, presumably right at the stroke of midnight, Google Inc. unpersoned *CounterPunch*. They didn't send out a press release or anything. They just quietly removed it from the Google News aggregator. Not very many people noticed. This happened just as the "fake news" hysteria was being unleashed by the corporate media, right around the time *The Washington Post* published a neo-McCarthyite smear piece vicariously accusing *CounterPunch*, and a number of other publications, of being "peddlers of Russian propaganda."[1]

As I'm sure you'll recall, that astounding piece of "journalism" (which The *Post* was promptly forced to disavow with an absurd disclaimer but has refused to retract) was based on the claims of an anonymous website apparently staffed by a couple of teenagers and a formerly rabidly anti-communist, now rabidly anti-Putin think tank.

Little did most people know at the time that these were just the opening salvos in what has turned out to be an all-out crackdown on any and all forms of vocal opposition to the global corporate ruling classes and their attempts to quash the ongoing nationalist backlash against their neoliberal agenda.

Almost a year later, things are much clearer. If you haven't been following this story closely, and you care at all about freedom of the press, freedom of speech, and that kind of stuff, you may want to take an hour or two and catch up a bit on what's been happening.

---

1 Timberg, Craig, "Russian propaganda effort helped spread fake news during election, experts say," The Washington Post, November 24, 2016

I provided a few examples of some of the measures governments and corporations have been taking to stifle expressions of dissent in my latest essay in *CounterPunch*,[2] and there are numerous more detailed articles online, like Andre Damon's piece from July,[3] and the follow-up he published last week (which reports that Pulitzer Prize-winning journalist and author Chris Hedges has also been unpersoned).[4] Or, if you're the type of person who only believes what corporations tell you, and who automatically dismisses anything published by a Trotskyist website, there was an article in December in *The Guardian*,[5] and a recent op-ed in *The New York Times*,[6] both of which at least reported what Google, Twitter, and Facebook are up to. Or you could read the latest by Robert Parry,[7] who also has "legitimate" (i.e., corporate) credentials, and who hasn't been unpersoned just yet, although I'm sure they'll get around to him eventually.

I am using the Orwellian verb "unperson" playfully, but I'm also trying to be precise. What's happening isn't censorship, technically, at least not in the majority of cases. While there *are* examples of classic censorship (e.g., in the U.K., France, and Germany), apart from so-called "terrorist content," most governments aren't formally banning expressions of anti-corporatist dissent. This isn't Czechoslovakia, after all. This is global capitalism, where the repression of dissent is a little more subtle.

The point of Google unpersoning *CounterPunch* (and many other publications) and Pulitzer Prize-winning journalists like Hedges is not to prevent them from publishing their work or otherwise render them invisible to readers. The goal is to delegitmize them, and thus decrease traffic to their websites and articles, and ultimately drive them out of business, if possible.

---

2 *"Tomorrow Belongs to the Corporatocracy," CounterPunch, October 20, 2017*

3 *Damon, Andre and Niemuth, Niles, "New Google algorithm restricts access to left-wing, progressive web sites," World Socialist Website, July 27, 2017*

4 *Damon, Andre, "Google escalates blacklisting of left-wing web sites and journalists," World Socialist Website, October 20, 2017*

5 *Solon, Olivia, "Facebook, Twitter, Google and Microsoft team up to tackle extremist content," The Guardian, December 6, 2016*

6 *Klonick, Kate, "The Terrifying Power of Internet Censors," The New York Times, September 13, 2017*

7 *Parry, Robert, "Russia-gate Breeds 'Establishment McCarthyism'," Consortium News, October 26, 2017*

Another objective of this non-censorship censorship is discouraging writers like myself from contributing to publications like *CounterPunch*, *Truthdig*, *Alternet*, *Global Research*, and any other publications the corporatocracy deems "illegitimate." Google unpersoning a writer like Hedges is a message to other non-ball-playing writers. The message is, "this could happen to you." This message is meant for other journalists, primarily, but it's also aimed at writers like myself who are making a living (to whatever degree) writing and selling what we think of as "literature."

Yes, as you've probably guessed by now, in addition to writing political satire, I am (as rogue journalist Caitlin Johnstone so aptly put it once) an "elitist wanker." I've spent the majority of my adult life writing stage plays and working in the theater, and it doesn't get any more elitist than that. My plays are published by "establishment" publishers, have won a few awards, and have been produced internationally. I recently published my "debut novel" (which is what you call it if you're an elitist wanker) and am currently trying to promote and sell it. I mention this, not to blow my little horn, but to set the stage to try to illustrate how these post-Orwellian intimidation tactics (i.e., unpersoning people from the Internet) work. These tactics do not just suppress information. They enforce conformity at a much deeper level.

The depressing fact of the matter is, in our brave new Internet-dominated world, corporations like Google, Twitter, and Facebook (not to mention Amazon) are, for elitist wankers like myself, in the immortal words of Colonel Kurz, "either friends or they are truly enemies to be feared." If you are in the elitist wanker business, regardless of whether you're Jonathan Franzen, Garth Risk Hallberg, Margaret Atwood, or some "mid-list" or "emerging" author, there is no getting around these corporations.

So it's kind of foolish, professionally speaking, to write a bunch of essays that will piss them off, and then publish these essays in *CounterPunch*. Literary agents advise against this. Other elitist literary wankers, once they discover what you've been doing, will avoid you like the bubonic plague. Although it's perfectly fine to write books and movies about fictional evil corporations, writing about how real corporations are using their power to mold societies into self-policing virtual prisons of politically correct, authoritarian consumers is ... well, it's something that is just not done in professional elitist wanker circles.

Normally, all this goes without saying, as these days most elitist wankers are trained how to write, and read, and think, in MFA conformity factories, where they screen out any unstable weirdos with unhealthy interests in political matters. This is to avoid embarrassing episodes like Harold Pinter's Nobel Prize lecture[8] (which, if you haven't read it, you probably should), and is why so much of contemporary literature is so well-behaved and instantly forgettable.

This institutionalized screening system is also why the majority of journalists employed by mainstream media outlets understand, without having to be told, what they are, and are not, allowed to report. Chomsky explains how this system operates in "What Makes Mainstream Media Mainstream."[9] It isn't a question of censorship; the system operates on rewards and punishments, financial and emotional coercion, and subtler forms of intimidation. Making examples of non-cooperators is a particularly effective tactic. Ask any one of the countless women whose careers have been destroyed by Harvey Weinstein, or anyone who's been to graduate school, or worked at a major corporation.

Or let me provide you with a personal example.

A couple weeks ago, I googled myself (which we elitist wankers are wont to do), and noticed that two of my published books had disappeared from the "Knowledge Panel" in the upper right section of the search results. I also noticed that the people "People Also Search For" in the panel had changed. For years, consistently, the people you saw there had been various other elitist literary wankers and leftist political types. Suddenly, they were all rather right-wing types, people like Ilana Mercer, John Derbyshire, and other VDARE writers. So that was a little disconcerting.

I set out to contact the Google Search specialists to inquire about this mysterious development, and was directed to a series of unhelpful web pages directing me to other unhelpful pages with little boxes where you can write and submit a complaint to Google, which they

8 Pinter, Harold, "Art, Truth & Politics," 2005, available online at www.nobelprize.org.

9 Chomsky, Noam, "What Makes Mainstream Media Mainstream," Z Magazine, October 1997

will completely ignore. Being an elitist literary wanker, I also wrote to Google Books, and exchanged a number of cordial emails with an entity (let's call her Ms. O'Brien) who explained that, for "a variety of reasons," the "visibility" of my books (which had been consistently visible for many years) was subject to change from day to day, and that, regrettably, she couldn't assist me further, and that sending her additional cordial emails was probably a pointless waste of time. Ms. O'Brien was also pleased to report that my books had been restored to "visibility," which, of course, when I checked, they hadn't.

"Whatever," I told myself, "this is silly. It's probably just some IT thing, maybe Google Books updating its records, or something." However, I was still perplexed by the "People Also Search For" switcheroo, because it's kind of misleading to link my writing to that of a bunch of serious right-wingers. Imagine, if you were a dystopian sci-fi fan, and you googled me to check out my book and see what else I had written, and so on, and my Google "Knowledge Panel" popped up and displayed all these far-right VDARE folks. Unless you're a far-right VDARE type yourself, that might be a little bit of a turn-off.

At that point, I wondered if I was getting paranoid. Because Google Search runs on algorithms, right? And my political satire and commentary is published, not only in *CounterPunch*, but also in *The Unz Review*, where these far-right-wing types are also published. Moreover, my pieces are often reposted by what appear to be "Russia-linked" websites, and everyone knows that the Russians are all a bunch of white supremacists, right? On top of which, it's not like I'm Stephen King here. I am hardly famous enough to warrant the attention of any post-Orwellian corporate conspiracy to stigmatize anti-establishment dissent by manipulating how authors are displayed on Google (i.e., subtly linking them to white supremacists, anti-Semites, and others of that ilk).

So, okay, I reasoned, what probably happened was, over the course of twenty-four hours, for no logical reason whatsoever, all the folks who had been googling me (along with other leftist and literary figures) suddenly stopped googling me, all at once, while, more or less at the exact same time, hundreds of right-wingers started googling me (along with those white supremacist types they had, theoretically, already been googling). That kind of makes sense when you think about it, right? I mean, Google couldn't be doing this intentionally. It must have been some sort of algorithm that detected this sudden, seismic shift in the demographic of people googling me.

Or, I don't know, does that possibly sound like a desperate attempt to rationalize the malicious behavior of an unaccountable, more or less godlike global corporation that wields the power of life and death over my book sales and profile on the Internet (a more or less godlike global corporation that could do a lot of additional damage to my sales and reputation with complete impunity once the piece you're reading is published)? Or am I simply getting paranoid, and, in fact, I've developed a secret white supremacist fan base without my knowledge? Only Google knows for sure.

Such are the conundrums elitist literary wankers have to face these days … that is, those of us wankers who haven't learned to keep our mouths shut yet. Probably the safest course of action, regardless of whether I'm being paranoid or Google does have me on some kind of list, is to lay off the anti-corporatist essays, and definitely stop contributing to *CounterPunch*, not to mention *The Unz Review*, and probably also give up the whole dystopian satire novel thing, and ensure that my second novel conforms to the "normal" elitist wanker rules (which every literary wanker knows, but which, technically, do not exist). Who knows, if I play my cards right, maybe I can even sell the rights to Miramax, or … okay, some other corporation.

Once that happens, I assume that Google will promptly restore me to normal personhood, and return my books to "visibility," and I will ride off into the Hollywood sunset with the Clintons, Clooneys, and Pichais, and maybe even Barack Obama himself, if he isn't off jet skiing with Richard Branson, or having dinner with Jeff and MacKenzie Bezos, who just happen to live right down the street, or hawking the TPP on television. By that time, *CounterPunch* and all those other "illegitimate" publications will have been forced onto the dark web anyway, so I won't be giving up all that much. I know, that sounds pretty cold and cynical, but my liberal friends will understand … I just hope all my new white supremacist fans will find it in their hearts to forgive me.

The Year of the Headless Liberal Chicken

December 8, 2017

According to the Chinese zodiac, 2017 has been the Year of the Rooster. Myself, I've decided to designate it the Year of the Headless Liberal Chicken. I don't mean that to be insulting … or, all right, I guess I do, a little. But my heart goes out to liberals, seriously. At this point, the amount of utterly baseless, contradictory propaganda, mass hysteria, and just flat-out insanity the ruling classes have demanded they swallow is more than any human mind, no matter how medicated, could possibly handle. Is it any wonder so many of them have lost it and started seeing Nazis and Russians coming out of the woodwork? Just consider what the average liberal has been forced to try to cognitively reconcile since the tragic events of last November.

First came the overwhelming shock of Hillary Clinton's loss to Trump, a repulsive, word-salad-babbling buffoon with absolutely no political experience who the media had been portraying to liberals as the Second Coming of Adolf Hitler. This was a candidate, let's recall, who jabbered about building a "beautiful wall" to protect us from the hordes of "Mexican rapists" and other "bad hombres" who were invading America, and who had boasted about grabbing women "by the pussy" like a prepubescent 6th grade boy. While he had served as a perfect foil for Clinton, and had provided hours of entertainment in a comic-book-villain kind of way, the prospect of a Donald Trump presidency was inconceivable in the minds of liberals. So, when it happened, it was like the Martians had invaded.

Mass hysteria gripped the nation. There was beaucoup wailing and gnashing of teeth. Liberals began exhibiting irrational and, in some cases, rather disturbing behaviors. Many degenerated into dissociative states and just sat there with their phones for hours obsessively reloading the popular vote count, which Clinton had won, on FiveThirtyEight. Others festooned themselves with safety pins and went out looking for defenseless minorities who they could "demonstrate solidarity" with.[1] Owen Jones flew in from London to join his colleague Steven Thrasher, who was organizing a guerilla force to resist "the normalization of Trump"[2] and the global race war he was about to launch, which "not all of us were going to get out of alive."

In the weeks immediately following the election, the mainstream media inundated liberals with pronouncements of the advent of an "Age of Darkness"[3] and the "Triumph of White Supremacy"[4] over the beneficent values of globalism. Yes, it was pretty much the end of everything.[5] America was facing nothing less than a descent into "racial Orwellianism,"[6] "Zionist anti-Semitism,"[7] and "the bottomless pit of Fascism" itself.[8] Liberals, who by then had dispensed with the safety pins, immediately set about terrorizing their children with visions of the impending holocaust,[9] which would be carried out by the genocidal, racist monsters who had voted for Trump.[10]

At that point, the media had been hammering hard on the Trump-is-Hitler narrative for months, so they had to stick with that for a while. It had only been a few weeks, after all, since *The Wall Street Journal*, *The New York Times*, *The Washington Post*, *The Guardian*, and

---

1 *Abad-Santos, Alex, "A small way to show solidarity after Donald Trump's presidential win, inspired by Brexit," Vox, November 14, 2016*

2 *Thrasher, Steven W., "Don't let Donald Trump become the new normal," The Guardian, November 14, 2016*

3 *Freedland, Jonathan, "If Donald Trump wins, it'll be a new age of darkness," The Guardian, November 4, 2016*

4 *Mason, Paul, "Globalisation is dead, and white supremacy has triumphed," The Guardian, November 9, 2016*

5 *Krugman, Paul, "How Republics End," The New York Times, December 19, 2016*

6 *Blow, Charles M., "Trump: Making America White Again," The New York Times, November 21, 2016*

7 *Gjelten, Tom, "Could A Trump Presidency Be Pro-Israel And White Nationalist At The Same Time?" National Public Radio (Morning Edition), November 21, 2016*

8 *Olberman, Keith, "The Resistance with Keith Olberman," GQ, November 16, 2016 (available on Youtube at: https://www.youtube.com/watch?v=RNcji9CknMs)*

9 *Sorkin, Aaron, "Read the Letter Aaron Sorkin Wrote His Daughter After Donald Trump Was Elected President," Vanity Fair, November 9, 2016*

10 *Bouie, Jamelle, "There's No Such Thing as a Good Trump Voter," Slate, November 15, 2016*

numerous other establishment publications, had explained how Trump was using special fascist code words like "global elites," "international banks," and "lobbyists" to signal his virulent hatred of the Jews to the millions of Americans who, according to the media, were secretly Hitler-loving fascists.

This initial post-election propaganda was understandably somewhat awkward, as the plan had been to be able to celebrate the "Triumph of Love over the Forces of Hate," and the demise of the latest Hitlerian bogeyman. But this was the risk the ruling classes took when they chose to Hitlerize Trump, which they wouldn't have done if they'd thought for a moment that he had a chance of actually winning the election. That's the tricky thing about Hitlerizing people. You need to be able to kill them, eventually. If you don't, when they turn out not to be Hitler, your narrative kind of falls apart, and the people you've fear-mongered into a frenzy of frothing, self-righteous fake-Hitler-hatred end up feeling like a bunch of dupes who'll believe anything the government tells them. This is why, normally, you only Hitlerize foreign despots you can kill with impunity. This is Hitlerization 101 stuff, which the ruling classes ignored in this case, which the left poor liberals terrified that Trump was actually going to start building Trump-branded death camps and rounding up the Jews.

Fortunately, just in the nick of time, the ruling classes and their media mouthpieces rolled out the "Russian Propaganda" story. *The Washington Post* (whose owner's multimillion dollar deal with the CIA, of course, has absolutely no effect on the quality of its journalism) led the charge with a McCarthyite smear job,[11] legitimizing the baseless allegations of some random website and a think tank staffed by professional charlatans like Clint Watts, a self-appointed "Russia expert"[12] who appears not to speak a word of Russian or have any other "Russia expert" credentials, but is available both for television and Senate Intelligence Committee appearances. Numerous similar smear pieces followed. Liberals breathed a big sigh of relief … that

11 Timberg, Craig, "Russian propaganda effort helped spread fake news during election, experts say," The Washington Post, November 24, 2016

12 Blumenthal, Max, "McCarthyism Inc.: Hyping the Russian Threat to Undermine Free Speech," Alternet, November 13, 2017 (The charlatan in question being Clint Watts, "a former U.S. Army officer who had branded himself an expert on Russian meddling.")

Hitler business had been getting kind of scary. How long can you go, after all, with Hitler stumbling around the White House before somebody has to go in there and shoot him?

In any event, by January, the media were playing down the Hitler stuff and going balls-out on the "Russiagate" story. According to *The Washington Post* (which, let's remember, is a serious newspaper, as opposed to a propaganda organ of the so-called U.S. "Intelligence Community"), not only had the Russians "hacked" the election, but they had hacked the Vermont power grid! Editorialists at *The New York Times* were declaring that Trump "had been appointed by Putin," and that the U.S.A. was now "at war" with Russia. This was also around the time when liberals first learned of the Trump-Russia Dossier, which detailed how Putin was blackmailing Trump with a video the FSB had shot of Trump and a bunch of Russian hookers peeing on a bed in a Moscow hotel in which Obama had allegedly slept.

This nonsense was reported completely straight-faced, and thus liberals were forced to take it seriously. Imagine the cognitive dissonance they suffered. It was like that scene in *1984* when the Party abruptly switches enemies, and the war with Eurasia becomes the war with Eastasia. Suddenly, Trump wasn't Hitler anymore. Now he was a Russian sleeper agent who Putin had been blackmailing into destroying democracy with this incriminating "golden showers" video. Putin had presumably been "running" Trump since Trump's visit to Russia in 2013 to hobnob with "Russia-linked" Russian businessmen and attend the Miss Universe pageant in Moscow. During the ensuing partying, Trump must have gotten loaded on Diet Coke and gotten carried away with those Russian hookers. Now, Putin had him by the short hairs and was forcing him to staff his Manchurian cabinet with corporate CEOs and Goldman Sachs guys, who probably had also been videotaped by the FSB in Moscow hotels paying hookers to pee on furniture ... or performing whatever other type of seditious, perverted kink they were into.

Before the poor liberals had time to process this, the ruling classes launched "the Resistance." You remember the Pussyhat People, don't you? And the global corporate PR campaign which accompanied their historic "Women's March" on Washington? Do you remember liberals like Michael Moore shrieking for the feds to arrest Donald Trump? Or publications like *The New York Times*, *Salon*, and many others, and even State Satirist Stephen Colbert accusing Trump and anyone who supported him of treason … a crime, let's recall, that is punishable by death? Do you remember folks like William Kristol and Rob "the Meathead" Reiner demanding that the "deep state" launch a coup against Trump to rescue America from the Russian infiltrators?

Ironically, the roll-out of this "Russiagate" hysteria was so successful that it peaked too soon, and prematurely backlashed all over itself. By March, when Trump had not been arrested, nor otherwise removed from office, liberals, who by that time the corporate media had teased into an incoherent, throbbing state of anticipation were … well, rather disappointed.

By April, they were exhibiting all the hallmark symptoms of clinical psychosis. This mental breakdown was due to the fact that the media pundits and government spooks who had been telling them that Trump was Hitler, and then a Russian sleeper agent, were now telling them that he wasn't so bad, because he'd pointlessly bombed a Syrian airstrip, and dropped a $314 million Massive Ordnance Air Blast bomb on some alleged "terrorist caves" in Afghanistan.

As if liberals' poor brains weren't rattled enough, the corporate media then switched back to, first, the Russian Propaganda narrative (which they expanded into a global threat), then, the Hitler stuff again, but this time Trump wasn't actually Hitler, because Putin was Hitler, or at least he was fomenting Hitlerism throughout the West with his legions of fascist hacker bots who were "influencing" unsuspecting consumers with their blitzkrieg of divisive "fake news" stories. Oh, yeah, and now Putin had also done Brexit, or Trump and Robert Mercer had, but they were working for Putin, who had also hacked the French election that he hadn't hacked, or … whatever … this was no time to worry about what had or hadn't actually happened. The peace and prosperity President Obama had reestablished throughout the West by incessantly bombing the Greater Middle East and bailing out his pals at the Wall Street banks was being torn asunder by Vladimir Putin, who at some point had apparently metamorphosized from a ruthless, former KGB autocrat into a white supremacist megalomaniac.

Right on cue, on the weekend of August 11-12 in Charlottesville, Virginia, where there had never been any history of racism, a "national gathering" of approximately five hundred tiki-torch-bearing neo-Nazis, Ku Klux Klan types, and other white supremacists, many of them barking Nazi slogans, marched into the pages of history. Never before have so few fascists owed so much to the mainstream media, which showered them with overwrought coverage, triggering a national "Nazi" panic. Liberals poured into the streets, tearing down Confederate monuments, and otherwise signaling their total intolerance of the racism they had tolerated until a few days earlier. People named after Robert E. Lee, and horses named after General Lee's horse, went into hiding to until the panic subsided.

This was wise, as by then the so-called "anti-fascists" were showing up in force at anything resembling a right-wing rally and stomping the living Hitler out of Nazis, and Trump supporters, and journalists, and ... well, anyone they didn't think looked quite right. This totally preemptively self-defensive, non-violent type of violent behavior, naturally, shocked and horrified liberals, who are strongly opposed to all forms of violence that aren't carried out by the U.S. military, or the police, or someone else wearing a uniform. Unsure as to whom they were supposed to condemn, i.e., the Nazis or the Antifa terrorists, they turned for guidance to the corporate ruling classes, who informed them it was time to censor the Internet.

This made about as much sense as any of the other nonsense they'd been spoonfed so far, so liberals decided to get behind it, or at least look the other way while it happened. Facebook, Google, Amazon, Twitter (and all the other global corporations that control the Internet, the media, Hollywood, and every other means of representing "reality") surely have people's best interests at heart. Plus, they're only censoring the Nazis, and the terrorists, and the Russian "fake news" disseminators, and ... OK, a lot of leftist publications, and award-winning journalists, and anyone else espousing "divisive," anti-American, or anti-corporate, "extremist" views.

Look, I know what you're probably thinking, but it isn't like liberals don't really care about fundamental liberal values like freedom of the press and speech and all that. It's just that they desperately need the Democrats to take back the House and the Senate next year, so they can get on with impeaching Trump, and if they have to stand by while the corporations suppress a little leftist dissent, or, you know, transform the entire Internet into a massive, mind-numbing echo chamber of neo-McCarthyite corporate conformity … well, sacrifices have to be made.

This can't go on forever, after all ... this level of full-blown mass hysteria can only be sustained for so long. It's all fine and good to be able to whip people up into a frenzied mob, but at some point you need to have an endgame.

The neoliberal ruling classes know this. Their endgame is actually fairly simple. Their plan is to (a) make an example of Trump to discourage any future billionaire idiots from screwing with their simulation of democracy, and (b) demonize anyone deviating from neoliberal ideology as a fascist, a racist, an anti-Semite, or otherwise "abnormal" or "extremist." Their plan is *not* to incinerate the entire planet in a war with Russia. We're not on the brink of World War III (despite how many Twitter likes or Facebook shares it might get me to say that). Yes, eventually, they want to force Russia to return to the kind of "cooperation" it engaged in during the 1990s, when it was run by an incorrigible drunkard and the Goldman Sachs boys and their oligarch pals were looting the country for all it was worth … but that has little to do with all this.

No, the corporate ruling classes' endgame here is to reestablish neoliberal "normality," so we can get back to the War on Terror (or whatever they'll be calling it by then), and put this "neo-nationalist revolt against neoliberalism" episode behind us. To do that, they will need to install some sort of hopey-changey, Obama-like messiah, or at least somebody who can play the part of POTUS like a normal person and not sit around the Oval Office gobbling McDonald's and retweeting racist memes by random British fascists.

The way things are going, that might take a while, but rest assured they'll get there eventually. Now that Robert Mueller has proved that Trump colluded with Vladimir Putin by obstructing an investigation by Comey into Michael Flynn's lying to the FBI about not colluding with the Russian ambassador on behalf of Israel at Kushner's behest, the dominoes are surely about to fall.

Once they all have, and Donald Trump's head has been mounted on a spike on the White House lawn as a warning to any other potential usurpers, all this Russia and Nazi hysteria that has the poor liberals running around like headless chickens will disappear. Russia will go back to being Russia. The North American Nazi Menace, deprived of daily media coverage, will go back to being a fringe phenomenon. Liberals will go back to ignoring politics (except identity politics, naturally) and obediently serving the global capitalist ruling elites that are destroying the planet, and the lives of millions of human beings, in order to increase their profit margins. Sure, there'll be a brief emotional hangover, once the adrenaline rush wears off and they look back at their tweets and Facebook posts, which in hindsight might convey the impression that they spent the better part of a year parroting whatever insane propaganda the corporate media pumped out at them, and otherwise behaving like Good Americans ... but then, that's what the "delete" key is for.

Acknowledgements

Many thanks to Julie Blumenthal, Anthony Freda, Dan Zollinger, John Stauber, Jeffrey St. Clair, Ron Unz, Tony Sutton, Matt Taibbi, Diana Johnstone, Catte Black, Kit Knightly, Vaska Tumir, Patrice Greanville, Lissa Johnson, Carey Weeks, Adam C. Madison, Hannah Rush, Maria Martinez, Shirley Fyfe, Nancy Volle, Flavia Westerwelle, J. David Bartram, Chris Farmer, Sage S. Johnston, Walter Broner, D. J. Richard, Sergey Zolotarev, Annette Baca, Michael McKay, Mark Brown, Judy Meinhold, Meredith McElroy, Philip Baldwin, Stella Ai, Anahita Mobarhan, Teri Cento, Jaap Greijdanus, D.C. MacKenzie, Paul Randall, Neil MacLeod, Alan Hodge, Alexis Viera, Don Gates, Zach Wheat, Blair Cummings, Kelley Lane, Colin McEvoy, Marjaleena Repo, S. A. Black, Kristin Kaul, Vernon Van Steenkist, Sean Hyland, John Bevan, David Marshall, Caitlin Johnstone, Robert Laine, Trina Shirk, Nico Dietel, John Bartram, Colleen McGuire, John Doores, Reg Tydell, Raymond Munro, Rob Murray, Eric Rasmussen, Van Foreman, Dimitrij Petkowski, Corey Twinney, Louis Haywood, Kenneth Goodman, Suellen Beverly, Kurtis Overkamp, Sean Carnohan, Andy Ward, Andrew Moynihan, John Read, Peter LaTona, Stan Smith, Kate Kasserman, Sharon F. Crawford, Andrew Ward, Marjorie Mannos, Kurt Weithaler, Alan Rojer, Daniel Wirt, James Williamson, Josh Silver, Susie Kneedler, Fritz the Cat, Michael Denny, Susan Tinsley, Elliot Chen, Robert Kaplan, Kenneth Goodman, ZeroHedge, Entelekheia, Tlaxcala, Oriente Mídia, ZNet, Burbuja, The Fringe News, Vocidallestero, Public Reading Rooms UK, Agora Vox, Belligerent Act, and everyone else who published, translated, and otherwise supported the publication of these essays.

C. J. Hopkins is an award-winning playwright, novelist and political satirist. His plays have been produced and have toured internationally, playing theatres and festivals including Riverside Studios (London), 59E59 Theaters (New York), Belvoir St. Theatre (Sydney), Traverse Theatre (Edinburgh), the Du Maurier World Stage Festival (Toronto), Needtheater (Los Angeles), 7 Stages (Atlanta), English Theater Berlin, the Edinburgh Festival Fringe, Adelaide Fringe, the Brighton Festival, and the Noorderzon Festival (the Netherlands). His playwriting awards include the 2002 Best of the Scotsman Fringe Firsts (*Horse Country)*, the 2004 Best of the Adelaide Fringe (*Horse Country*), and a 2005 Scotsman Fringe First (*screwmachine/eyecandy*). His plays are published by Bloomsbury Publishing/Methuen Drama (UK) and Broadway Play Publishing, Inc. (US) His political satire and commentary has appeared on NPR Berlin, in *CounterPunch*, *The Unz Review*, *ColdType*, *OffGuardian*, and other political journals. His debut novel, *Zone 23*, is published by Snoggsworthy, Swaine & Cormorant.

Also by C. J. Hopkins ...

... a darkly comic dystopian satire about being human, all-too-human, featuring two of the most endearing and emotionally messed-up Anti-Social anti-heroes that have ever rebelled against the forces of Normality.

- Snoggsworthy, Swaine & Cormorant (available from most online booksellers, or from a physical bookstore near you)

"A brilliant dystopian satire worthy of a place alongside Orwell's 1984 and Huxley's Brave New World." — Vaughn Treude, Steampunk Desperado

"Hopkins' ferociously funny yarn is not just a satire on our ever-worsening techno-dystopia ... Zone 23 resonates with the great critiques of technological civilization." — Kevin Barrett, The Unz Review

"CJ Hopkins masterly depicts the scary, crazy state of advanced capitalist fascism we live in now. . . jacked up a good few notches." — Amazon

"... a head-on train crash between comedian/linguist George Carlin and science fiction writer Philip K. Dick." — Goodreads

"A piercing satire that cuts right to the genetically modified heart of our corporate-controlled world ... the millennials' 1984." — Amazon

www.ingramcontent.com/pod-product-compliance
Lightning Source LLC
LaVergne TN
LVHW010106170826
845678LV00012B/2262
* 9 7 8 3 9 8 2 1 4 6 4 0 9 *